# Little Old Yeovil

## Brendon Owen

A donation from the sale of this book will go to the Adam Stansfield Foundation.

The Gazebo Press

Published by The Gazebo Press
34, Bishopston, Montacute,
Somerset, TA15 6UU

Printed by  F.W.B. Printing Ltd., Wincanton
Manufactured in Great Britain

# ACKNOWLEDGEMENTS

Many, many thanks go to Martin Baker and his *Ciderspace* team for giving me free access and use of all of the archives that this wonderful Yeovil Town internet site has tucked away. If you wish to know anything about Yeovil since 1999 and of course the up to the minute news, www.Ciderspace.co.uk is the place for you. I put my hands up to any factual mistakes in this book. They are certainly not *Ciderspace's*.

Big thanks also to the Moderators of *The Green Room II* and to their diverse and interesting membership for allowing me to re-produce some of their views. If you wish to know what the fans are saying and perhaps would like to express your point of view, go to www.tgr2.co.uk.

I wish to say a big thank you to Mike Kuntz for his permission to use the marvellous photographs that he has taken. Others have been retrieved from Google and if copyright is claimed, acknowledgement will be made in any further re-print of his book.

Thanks to Lin, my wife, who believed that I had left home for some time while writing this book. I was actually locked away in the turret of the west wing with just my keyboard.

Thanks to my printers, F.W.B.Printing Ltd., Wincanton who were very helpful and efficient.

And finally, what can I say to Gary Johnson, Terry Skiverton, Darren Way and our fantastic football team, other than thanks guys. It's been great.

### By the same author

One From the Plough
Yeovil 'til I Die
Behind the Green Door

### About the author

He's a Yeovil Town fan through and through. Say no more.

# CONTENTS

# CHAPTER 1

# REMEMBER

Let's start with some deep breathing; after all it's not possible to look back to the climax of the 2012/13 season without becoming emotional. All the wows, the I don't believe it's happenings, the rollercoaster emotions, up, down, spinning around, those added six minutes at Wembley that went on for an eternity and then the bouncing, the hugging, the laughing, the crying, the pure joy of it all. The lack of oxygen to our brains that made us float in a hazy disbelief. One thing we knew was that we had done it. WE ARE GOING UP!

WE ARE IN THE CHAMPIONSHIP!

The Wembley sounds of thousands of supporters singing 'Yeovil True',' Stand Up if you Love Yeovil' and 'Hey Gary Johnson' are now an echo in our minds but it takes very little to ignite the passions, the sights, the taste and the feel of that beautiful sunny afternoon on the East side of the stadium. The sun shines on the righteous they say. It was certainly dark and shady on the West side for our opponents, Brentford.

While you are taking these deep breaths think about that giant arena filling with the green and white, the walk up Wembley Way, the flags, the shirts, the Little Old Yeovil banner.

Remember when the team ran out to warm up, the wall of noise that greeted them. Contrast that to the greeting that the Brentford players received, almost nothing from their yet to turn up fans. It must have given our lads a boost, an edge that they took into the first few minutes of play. Remember that sublime outside of the right foot strike by our Paddy. He had not scored for six games and then that!! You just knew he would, didn't you. Dan Burn rising like a giant at the back post and planting the second one in. Was it in? We couldn't tell for a split second and then ecstasy.

Remember very little about the second half except that, apart from once, we kept them out.

Don't forget unused substitute Gavin Williams' last kick for Yeovil Town when he back healed the ball from the touchline high into the crowd and got booked for his troubles.

That final whistle, that beautiful final whistle, that roar that ripped around the ground and blew the Brentford supporters away.

Think about Jamie McAllister, with his busted nose, lifting that shiny, shiny trophy with all of our boys high up in the stand bowing to receive their medals.

Remember Darren Way at the end when he skipped and leapt like a two year old. What a sight after all the pain and heartache he had been through.

Remember Garry Johnson when he almost let the trophy slip over the back of his head when he lifted it in triumph.

Remember Terry Skiverton punching the air with sheer delight.

Remember the beer at £4.80 a pint and no Thatcher's Gold!!

Spare a thought for those who could not be with us, Dad or Grandad who took us to our first Yeovil game and would be so proud of our Club's achievement and Adam Stansfield, our young hero from ten years before, so tragically cut down before his time and the tribute that was sung from the stands on 7 minutes.

As Bill Shankley said "Football's not a matter of life and death. It's more important than that!" No matter how mundane or exciting the rest of our lives turn out to be, that Wembley experience will etched on to our memories forever.  We are the chosen ones who can say that we were there. I am sure that like with the '49' Sunderland game the numbers who will claim that honour will steadily increase as the history of our great Club continues to expand.

So, how was it that we got there? Luck, chance, skill, preparation, who knows? Let's go back and see if it can be unravelled.  Even if it's not possible to put a finger on the exact reasons for success, it's a good excuse to relive some of the most interesting times in the history of Yeovil Town F.C. Our Club has reached the dizzy heights that few ever felt we could aspire to. We are in the second tier of the greatest football league in the world. AND WE DESERVE IT.

# CHAPTER 2

# THE DIM & DISTANT PAST

Often with great love stories, and let's face it we do have a love affair with Yeovil Town, it is necessary to go further back in time than might be thought to establish the germ of this grand relationship. Sometimes skeletons in the cupboard have to be rattled and maybe some unhappy times need to be aired just to compere and highlight the rapturous moments to come. So come with me and we will delve into what is now the dim and distant past.

By October 2011 Terry Skiverton had been Manager of the Club for a couple of seasons and with the help of Darren Way and Nathan Jones had managed to secure League One football despite their collective lack of experience, a tiny playing budget and an ever revolving door of short term loan players. To stay in the third tier was seen by many to be a great achievement but to others it felt that stagnation had set in and the Club had lost its ambition and was destined sooner rather than later to drop down into League Two.

The 2011/2012 season so far had not been a stonking success. Criticism was mounting as to the progress that Terry was making as a Manager. Many were becoming baffled by tactical decisions, substitutions, choice of loan players, no second goalkeeper, that sort of thing. Pretty usual stuff really when things are not going well.

To Yeovil fans Terry Skiverton would always be a hero. He had been a great player and an honest and true servant to Yeovil Town. He was thrust into management perhaps not at a time of his choosing, but hey who's going to turn down an opportunity when it presents itself. The fear was that his reputation was becoming somewhat tarnished.

Darren Way of course was held in the same esteem as Skivo, both being the backbone of our rise from the Non-League and forever in Yeovil folklore. The Club had been seen to be doing the right thing to appoint him as a coach , following his horrendous accident. To have dismissed him when he could no longer play would have been heartless but some voices were now being raised as to the benefits that Darren was bringing to the party.

Nathan Jones made up the third Musketeer in the management team. Not in the same league of adulation as Skivo and Weasel but a good player with years of experience who appeared to wear his heart on his sleeve. Surely able to bring valuable knowledge to the coaching team. But again rumblings of discontent were bouncing around the Huish Park faithful as to the effectiveness of Nathan's contribution.

After slumping 0-3 to Carlisle on the 15th October, the Internet site, *Ciderspace,* which was for many the first point of call for all things Yeovil Town, reported that:

'Yeovil Town manager Terry Skiverton has reiterated his calls for those at the club to 'stick together' as he attempts to get the Glovers out of trouble near the foot of the League One table. Following his post match interview that followed against Carlisle United, Skiverton has expressed concern at the level of booing aimed at his players after the game, and also that aimed at his assistant manager Nathan Jones.

Speaking to *BBC Somerset,* Skiverton believed that it was important that people were 'realistic' about the club's current situation and that they enjoyed the challenge of getting out of trouble:

"*I'm asking for the supporters to stick with us. There's a long way to go yet. We don't want to get cast adrift, but we've got to make sure that we're realistic. I keep repeating myself, but let's all stick together, and make sure that we climb this level and we climb this league, and get ourselves into a good position. But we can't do it with excuses, and we can't do it by feeling sorry for me, and we can't do it by saying 'poor me, poor me!' We've got to chalk this one off and really enjoy the challenge of the next game.*"'

On 21st October the poor run of form led Chairman John Fry to issue a statement about Skiverton and his management team in the *Western Gazette* and club site. Fry admitted that the last three weeks had been 'dismal' but made it clear he was still backing his manager:

"*This is not a time to panic. It is a time for everybody at the club from supporters to players and the board to stick together and turn things around as soon as possible. Last season Terry and his team finished in the second highest position in the history of the club. Terry's record has been very creditable during his tenure and he has not turned into a bad manager over the last few matches. Make no mistake, we will get over this dismal three weeks and come back stronger for the experience.*"

That's all we needed. The dreaded 'vote of confidence' from the Chairman. Where was this all leading to?

On 22nd October Yeovil slumped to the foot of the table after taking only a point in the 0-0 draw at Stevenage. That point was courtesy of a certain Marek Stech, a short term loan goalkeeper from West Ham who saved a penalty. Whatever became of him?

On the 25th another point but this time 2-2 at home to Leyton Orient.

On 29th October 2011 Terry Skiverton spoke to Ed Hadwin of BBC Bristol following a 0-1 defeat at Huish Park at the hands of Huddersfield Town. This was now the eleventh defeat of the season in all competitions, having flagged up only one win and four draws. He said
*"Some people might not like me, or like my methods and think that I'm not good enough, but the majority of the supporters do, and for them and the ones that are right behind us, we're just going to keep fighting away. One thing that I'm not going to do is to bow down to any challenge. I relish this. For us to turn this around will be a great achievement. We've done it before, and I'm telling you, and looking in your eye now, I will definitely do it again. ..... but listen, nothing gets me down. I'm over-positive; we keep on, we chalk that one off. We learn our lessons and we move on. We don't shirk from anything. One thing you can see with my team and my football club is that we're all together, and that 'Achieve By Unity' motto that's just under one of my pecs here will definitely get us out of trouble."*

The following day the draw for the 1st Round of the F.A. Cup was made. Would we get a home tie this time. The last time a ball with our number was drawn first was 3rd Round home to Liverpool in 2004. The law of averages was definitely in our favour this time. A good Cup run could do us the world of good. It might settle the team and stop the rot. Fans bit their nails as the velvet bag was tipped into the plastic gold fish bowl and the process began. Number 48 was what we wished to hear first, but no a certain Number 22 was plucked out straight away– Hereford United will play Number 48 – Yeovil Town. No!!! When cats had been kicked, wives and girlfriends abused and general order was restored, a fair number of supporters, having settled for always playing away, thought that taking on the old enemy wasn't such a bad thing. After all they were a division below us and also struggling. A trip to Edgar Street, with memories of that amazing 2nd Round replay in 1992 when winning 2-1set us up for a home tie with Arsenal, which many say saved our football club from going under, might be just the boost we now needed. Also the £18,200 prize money for Round 1would come in mighty handy.

For now it was back to League business on the following Saturday, 5th November. Not many fireworks as we took on fellow relegation fodder Chesterfield away and came back with a lucky point following a 2-2 draw.

Still bottom of the heap and three points adrift but we were looking forward to the F.A. Cup the next week. Well we were until Marek Stech got called up to the Czech Republic Under 21's who were to play in Armenia on the Friday afternoon. Much searching through the Atlas indicated that he was unlikely to be at Edgar Street by 3.00pm Saturday afternoon. Without a second string goalkeeper, Skivo drafted in the goalkeeper coach, Gareth Stewart, who had not played a competitive match at professional level since 1st March 2008. Interesting!

Fans on the *Green Room II*, the internet forum for those who wish to talk Yeovil Town at any time of the day or night were beginning to twitch. All shades of opinion were surfacing but one of the more perceptive comments was posted on 11th November 2011:
*As people, I don't think anyone has a problem with Terry, Nathan and Darren, they are all basically nice people but nice people don't win you football matches. They are committed to the club and passionate about the club, that is not in dispute but at the end of the day there is something wrong. We have the players capable but we are not getting the best out of them and the question has to be why? Although it is admirable that we stick with the three in the hope that it will come good how long do we have to give it before the reality sets in. A bit of guidance and experience is needed to help them at this present time and as said before if we were to bring in some help then there would probably not be room for all three of them and also I think there would be resentment. A decision needs to be made on what is best for the club. Stick with the three and hope it comes good or bite the bullet and bring someone in to help Terry.* (isistoleague)

~~~~~~~

Another was more succinct:
*One win in 16? managers have been sacked for less.* Stompe)

# CHAPTER 3

# A CERTAIN MR. JOHNSON

There was a God. 3-0 over Hereford and we marched on to Round 2 of the Cup. Relief all round, well temporarily. It just had to be a home draw this time. But no, away to Fleetwood Town of the Conference. Not many knew exactly where Fleetwood was, Hampshire?, Surrey sort of sounded right, but there it was up on the Fylde Coast of Lancashire, next door neighbour to Blackpool, 252 miles from Yeovil!
But meanwhile there was a forthcoming match to decide bragging rights in the region. Exeter City at home was coming up next and fingers were being crossed as to the outcome. Perhaps things were on the up.

Wrong! On 14th November *Ciderspace* announced 'Hammer Blow as Stech Leaves Yeovil Town'. He was recalled by his parent club, West Ham, who recently suffered their own problems with a loan goalkeeper, with Manuel Almunia being recalled by Arsenal. Stech made five appearances during his month long loan, putting in some superb performances along the way and so will be difficult to replace.

So while we read this news with a black cloud hanging overhead many would have been forgiven for missing another little item on the same day, namely that a certain Mr G. Johnson had parted company with League Two, Northampton Town. A 1-0 defeat at the hands of arch enemies, Luton Town, seemed to push the Board over the top. Their Chairman, David Cardoza said
*"Gary has been a successful manager in the past and I am sure he will be again in the future. Unfortunately, things just haven't worked out for Gary here, and there comes a point when you have to accept that fact, take stock and make a decision and following a discussion between Gary and I over the weekend, it was decided that we part company. We wish Gary all the very best for the future."*
*Ciderspace* went on to say that: He leaves them in 20th position in the League Two table, and three points above the relegation line. Gary had been in charge at Sixfields for just eight months.

Well poor old Gary. Who'd be a manager eh?

For those who did pick up on this item there was a little flurry of chat on the *Green Room II*:
*In my eyes, without being biased, I always rated him as a good manager. What's gone wrong? He seemed to get a fair amount of support at Northampton?* (like-a-glove)

~~~~~~~~~

*Amazing decline in his career since the 2008 play-off final.*
*2002: YTFC 3rd Conference, FA Trophy Winners*
*2003: 1st Conference*
*2004: 8th Div 3, FA Cup 3rd Round*
*2005: 1st League 2, FA Cup 4th Round*
*2006: BCFC League 1: from relegation fodder to 9th*
*2007: League 1: 2nd and promoted*
*2008: Championship: Top 6 all season, lost play-off final*
*2009: Championship: 10th*
*2010: Championship: Sacked whilst in 15th*
*2011: Fell out with owners at Peterborough, despite having them playing great football and being in a play-off spot. Sacked at Northampton with win % of just 20%.*
*The 'magic' from 2001 - 2008, with people talking of him as a Premier League (or even England) manager, soon forgotten.*
*Would you have him back? I would probably not.* (will_ran)

~~~~~~~~~

*Where next? I don't think the profile of our club currently is what he should be going for. He needs a club that is below where it should be, and that's certainly not us. Taking, and failing in a job so far down the leagues will have seriously hit his standing though, so he may find it much harder to cherry-pick an ideal job now. I don't know where next for him really.* (banio)

~~~~~~~

*Luton perhaps?* (will_ran)

~~~~~~~

*Or back to Cambridge?* (Unspeakable Cad)

~~~~~~~~~

*The big thing about GJ was he had a real affinity with the supporters they trusted him, he trusted them. Has he been a failure in the last two posts If leaving Peterboro in a play-off place is failure then only winning the league is success, did he have the same affinity with posh fans as Yeovil, no he didn't, same scenario at Northampton. As we all know it takes time to gain the trust of supporters not just 8 or 9 months maybe in the west*

*country we are a different breed, would he come back MOST DEFINITELY.*
(Frankie)

~~~~~~~~~

*He won't be coming back – I can't see JF wanting him back.* (Oracle)

They always say in football that you should never go back. Time and again this adage has been ignored and time and again it has ended in tears. We have only to look back a short time in Yeovil's history to see that the return for a second time of Brian Hall was less than successful. Gary, being a wise old sage, would surely not go against it. But just for a minute there must have been a surge of electricity coursing through Yeovil supporters. That crackle of excitement, that bolt out of the blue of hope and desire.

Ah well, back to all things League 1 and Huish Park. In fact the very next day, 15th November we heard some big news from the Chairman. Was it the purchase of more pegs to keep the tent (Marquee if you're posh) firmly in place? Perhaps another lean to at the back of the Home Stand for a drinking concourse? No, this was a lot more upbeat than that. This was talk of real bricks and mortar, a substantial development. No less than a whacking great supermarket to be built on the top training pitches. All singing, all dancing designs and drawings were to be displayed at a public exhibition later in the month so that we the fans and the neighbours on Abbey Manor could have a look and get excited about the future of the Club.

Chairman John Fry told the *Yeovil Express* that an architect would be present who could answer any questions supporters or other interested parties may have about the arrangements:
*"Yeovil Town FC is an important economic driver in the South West region and we are embarking on this project to ensure that the club has the resources and facilities on site to continue to compete in the Football League. By developing the area around the stadium we have the opportunity to bring investment to the club and the area. Feedback from the local community is key to the initial and ongoing success of this development. We look forward to meeting as many people as possible at the public exhibition as we seek to move forward with the proposals."*

Hang on a minute, what happened to the super duper new stand that was going to be built at the Copse Road end? Seems to have got missed off the plan. Still it was good to see something positive come from the Board. If they could get the 70,000 feet food store and 500 car park spaces and a little bit of community grass it would surely do the Club the world of good. They set out a project timetable with April/May 2012 the expected date for a determination of the application by the District Council. Building to start soon after and by the start of 2013/14 season we should be able to watch the match and then shoot up the aisles with a trolley for the celebration beers.

Still don't let's get carried away, we had the little matter of the local derby against Exeter on 19th November to think about.

Another draw 2-2, this time. Still it pushed us away from the bottom of the table. Were the fans happy? Some were, thinking that if only these draws could be turned into wins things would be ok. Others, all gloom and doom, calling for heads, Manager, Coach, Chairman, Kit man, anybody really just to relieve the pressure.

Andy Howard of the BBC asked Skivo after the match: "Off the bottom. Mentality-wise you say you want to edge clear. Does it make a difference not being at the bottom?"

Terry replied:

*No not really, because we've got to be ready. I think we've been very strong before, keeping everyone else above us. We've needed to be strong. But with that support behind us, and the mood that's within the camp, I'm still looking for us to beat 14th. It might be a bold statement of where we are at the moment, but we'll get to where we want to get to. It's just a matter of time.*

So it was just a matter of time. How much though the fans were asking. Talking of time, Chairman John Fry warned that if the Foodstore application were for some reason rejected" *It will be a struggle - a big struggle. In fact it will be dire, from the point of view that we have to bring in the revenues to maintain our position in the Football League. Basically, we are running out of time."* Not so good then John. Let's keep our fingers crossed and hope all goes well.

Next up was everyone's favourite away game, the 676 mile return trip to sunny Hartlepool. Still searching for the first away win of the season we only went and did it. 0-1. A Bondz N'Gala header on 25 minutes sent the 55 Yeovil fans home happy. Well it certainly took the pressure off the Manager and his coaches for a while.

Positive as ever Terry Skiverton talking after the match on 26th November said:
*We've threatened a clean sheet and at last we've done it. There was some good individual performances and the keeper came in and did well for us. It was all positives. Other teams will get dragged into the mix in the bottom half of the table in the New Year and we will get out of it."*

Onwards and upwards then and back to the glamour of the F.A.Cup. It was Friday 2nd December and we were on the telly. Because it was on ESPN and not many could watch in their homes, the Club threw open the tent so that we could gather together and cheer the Glovers on to victory over Fleetwood Town. Well that was the plan and to be fair the plan was working well up until the 82nd minute. 2-0 to Yeovil and then a couple of substitutions that caused
brows to furrow and before you knew it was 2-2 and last orders please. How that happened no one was really sure but at least we were still in the hat for Sunday's 3rd Round Draw and the replay to look forward to.

After the match ESPN spoke to Terry Skiverton:
*We had four or five decent chances that we would have normally put away to win this game but we didn't do it, so in that respect it is disappointing. We left ourselves too open at the back and gave away too much possession, and they put some decent pressure on us and came back, and I thought the equaliser was inevitable really. I thought it was a fantastic cup tie as the league side looked they would run away with it at first, and they pulled it back, so hopefully the game at our place will be another entertaining one for the fans."*

And what were the *Green Room II* forum fans saying about it?
*Well at least we are in the draw for a change, but this was one that clearly has got a way. Thought we were brilliant for the first 80 minutes with 10 men.*
*FFS how bad were Skiverton's subs tonight, have to agree with some posters on here he took off the two players that were keeping the ball for us.*
*It all depends on the draw now if this replay sparks into life.*
*Would have taken a draw before the game but we let them off big time or I should say Skivo did, way to negative last 10 minutes* (sedgy)
~~~~~~~~~
*And our gaffer played his career as a defender but we can't defend a lead. He is not strong enough to make the big decisions to drop senior players, or*

*have players playing in correct positions. Promote from the dressing room to boss rarely works.* (kmglover)

~~~~~~~~

*Fleetwood were woeful for 90% of the game, booting it out of play etc. We should have nothing to worry about for the replay. After all the hype they were lucky to get a replay and it should be another tv money spinner for us.* (sheffieldglover)

~~~~~~~~

*In all my dealings with Skivo I would say he is as sharp as a tack.* (Lector)

~~~~~~~~

*42" plasma tv's all around their* (Fleetwood Town) *supporters bar and even in the toilets was mentioned tonight. Poor old league 1 team has 200 people in a moldy tent watching 1 42" tv supplied by the funs,*
*Still............................ It could of been 250 unlucky fans if they had sold out.*
(Rock and Roll)

~~~~~~~~

*Yeovil or Fleetwood v Manchester United/City/Chelsea....*
*That should get a good crowd for the replay in....*
*I just hope and pray it's not home to Blackpool as there would be a huge incentive for Fleetwood to beat us.*
*They are a decent side who didn't give up. They are quite capable of embarrassing us* (Wurzel )

Talk about prophetic! Wurzel can I tap you for the next set of Lottery numbers? Came the Sunday afternoon draw for Round 3 and lo and hold, Blackpool at home for the lucky winners of the replay! You couldn't make it up. Of course Fleetwood now had everything to play for with the prospect of a full house for the visit of their illustrious neighbours. For us? Well £27,000 for winning the replay and also a big crowd at Huish Park and for revenge against the Tangerines for our defeat at their hands at Wembley in 2007. Also, it was going to be on the T.V. again. A chance for our boys to shine. Should be incentive enough surely?
Talking of prize money *Ciderspace* did a few calculations and reckoned that we had profited to the tune of £126,500 so far from the Cup. Just shows that if you can stick in there for a couple or three rounds the rewards are quite considerable.

Despite the good financial news there was a growing feeling of frustration among the fans and in some camps the need for a wholesale change of management. Perhaps as a follower of the *Green Room II* Terry Skiverton seemed to be well aware of the current vibes. Speaking to *PA Sport* the gaffer said:

*"It's a case of being patient and making sure that we don't get overly frustrated and don't get caught up in the whole Premier League way of looking at things where, if you go on a run of defeats, the manager has got to go, the board has got to go and then you've got to get a big name in that doesn't care for the club. All of a sudden you turn into that topsy-turvy world where you end up getting relegated, then you end up with the club getting in trouble and then you end up with supporters not having a club to support. One thing that we do here is that we're very strong, we stick together and we compete well and we do it in a fair way."*

After 19 games played, Yeovil were 22nd in the League One table with 16 points gained, as they went into that Saturday's home game against Notts County. The points tally was identical to their situation the previous season, although at that time they sat on the bottom of the table, six points adrift of safety. Skiverton believed that coming into the halfway point of the season that his team were capable of achieving the same again:

*"We were there last year and everybody was saying the same thing and we ended up finishing 14th and we finished above Sheffield Wednesday and on the same points as Charlton. So do I think we can finish 14th again? Of course I do. But we have to make sure we do it at the right time. I know where we're going to get to and the difference between seeing the big picture and being worried about ourselves is that we've got to enjoy every day without worrying about what's going to happen in the future."*

Saturday 10th December Yeovil climbed out of the relegation zone with a 1-0 win over promotion chasing Notts County. Described by *Ciderspace* as a scrappy, low quality game, probably most fans would have delighted with the 88th minute winner from substitute Andy Williams. After all, a win is a win, is a win. And a win could surely only boost the team in advance of the F.A. Cup replay coming up on the following Tuesday night, 13th December.

Terry speaking to BBC Bristol after the match said:

*"I think we might be just above the relegation zone? So it's another positive for everybody at the club. We've got an FA Cup game here on Tuesday. I've just walked into this media room and there seems to be a queue outside which I've not seen very often in my last few years of being at the club, and maybe they've got a little bit of a buzz for the FA Cup now. We can now turn*

*our attentions to that. From it being a real disappointing first half (of the season) it seems that the momentum is picking up for us."*

Six games unbeaten, moving in the right direction up the league, still in the F.A. Cup, things were on the up.......weren't they?
Writers on the *Green Room II* in the hours leading up the replay were saying complimentary things about Skivo:

*backing Skivo all the way*
*I think it's nice for a change that we get a player turned into a manager!*
*Skivo has pride and spirit for the club of Yeovil town and we should all get behind him, Nathan and Darren*! (welsh glover)

~~~~~~~~

*He's not perfect, he has many faults. But time and time again he's managed to turn things around when things were looking dire. I think he deserves credit for that.* (Rich the Glover)

~~~~~~~~

*....I'm with you all the way with supporting Skivo and his team.*(daveyboy)

The Tuesday night arrived, 3276 gathered at Huish Park, including 290 Fleetwood fans, courtesy of free coaches from Lancashire (Worth making a note of that for the future Yeovil). T.V. cameras were rolling, the Huish faithfully were ready and then the wheels came off! Yeovil Town were indescribably bad. Fleetwood were all over them like a rash. They just waltzed round us, through us and over us. 2-0 and away up the motorway they raced to their destiny with Blackpool. Back at Huish Park the 'faithful' gave full vent to their feelings as the team were forced by Skivo to applaud the crowd. The open derision and booing probably reached an all time record at the ground. And to be fair, it was much deserved. Some of the players were not fit to wear the shirt.
In fairness to Terry he stepped out in front of the ESPN cameras and took it on the chin. Despite the huge disappointment that was written across his face he graciously gave credit to Fleetwood Town, saying:
*"I think that one team really wanted it. They had a little more incentive and they seemed to hammer that home to us tonight. As poor as we were, I think Fleetwood played very well. You've got to give them all the credit. I've been on the other side of the fence and the other changing room with Yeovil in the past. I've really got to apologise to my supporters for that first half performance. We were dreadful. For how well we've done in recent league*

*form, we turn up tonight and we don't show our home fans that passion, that commitment and that determination."*

*Ciderspace* reported: ' In the end Yeovil got what they deserved, and Fleetwood got what they deserved - a home tie against Fylde coast neighbours Blackpool. This wasn't a non-league side playing backs-to-the-wall football to scrape out a jammy win. This was a side who outclassed a team two leagues above them, and turned them into a petulant and often disorganised side who were outplayed in midfield....... A poor showing tonight, and made all the worse by it being witnessed by the television cameras.'

Terry Skiverton then spoke to BBC Bristol:

*"We played like a team that's looking to get relegated. That's just not acceptable. I'm very disappointed tonight. We're going to go over it now. I've got a meeting booked in with them for ten o'clock, and we need to put a few things right, because I can't let this sit on my chest tonight. We're going to deal with it tomorrow as we're going to have to have another meeting tomorrow. I've got to get in there and find out how badly we really did play."*

Well the fans knew how badly they played. The *Green Room II* was awash with opinion:

*The result wasn't the shock but the performance and lack of pride and ability was.*(Pager)

~~~~~~~

*outclassed it says in parts on the official website .*(sedgy)

~~~~~~~

*That'll be the part between the game starting and ending.* (Jack Adams)

~~~~~~~

*Out played in parts, can someone explain which part we were better in then. This is supposed to be Skivos team, well say no more.* (Breno 1954)

~~~~~~~

*How many times can he apologise over and over for the same mistakes.. and yet change and correct nothing? Sorry Skivo but you're either stubborn and/or you simply haven't got a clue what to do. I'm going with both.* (nobrakes)

~~~~~~~

*I have backed our management team for a long time, but tonight's performance has been the final straw.*
*Tonights preformance was shambolic, possibly the worst all season.*
*The players and management should be ashamed.*
*We need someone who can come in and bring the best out of the players, Skivo and Jonesy for me have lost that ability and need to go before it's too late.* (MRB)

~~~~~~~~~

*Can't believe what I saw tonight - how long is it going to be allowed go on?*(RiffRaff)

~~~~~~~

*The forum has gone ballistic tonight not surprisingly after a truly awful performance.*
*The problem is what can we do as fans.*
*Skivo clearly is not up to being a football manager but as always the blame lies at JF'S door.* (valetta baby)

~~~~~~~

*Leave you with this... You know it's been a bad night at the office when you can put up a serious case for your goalkeeping coach being your man of the match.* (ToggsYTFC)

The last word on what was a hideous night had to go to Terry Skiverton. Talking to BBC Somerset two days later when some of the dust had settled:
*"On reflection since I've taken over, that's the worst we've played. That's even from when I first took over. These things do happen, and again I'll apologise to the supporters. We'll put it into the archives and we have to learn from it, and that's one thing that we need to do as a team............We gave them a day off (on Wednesday) to relax and recover, and then this morning (Thursday) we've come in like it didn't even happen. I think that's the way that we've got to look at it."*

*Ciderspace* reported on 18th December that: 'Yeovil Town manager Terry Skiverton has revealed that he had a meeting with Chairman John Fry in the wake of the club's shock FA Cup exit. In the fall-out of the defeat against Fleetwood Town, the Glovers first team boss and Chairman sat down to discuss the future direction of the club, including Fry's expectations moving forward.'

Not too surprisingly, Skivo did not reveal to *BBC Somerset* what sort of things were discussed, but he admitted that he had been told 'in no uncertain terms' the expectations upon him as a manager

*"I really want to prove to our home supporters and our home fans that we are a good side. I sat down this week and I had a very long and fruitful meeting with the Chairman. It was a strong meeting, and in no uncertain terms the Chairman has told me the way he wants the club to move forward, and I accept that.*

*It was just a really good meeting for me to realise that I can't take my foot off the gas, and nights like Tuesday definitely can't happen. I've still got that in my head, and it makes me even more determined now to prove to our supporters that we can climb that table and that we can get to where we want to get to. I definitely know that I'll make it up to them."*

Oh and a 0-0 draw at Rochdale almost slipped past unnoticed on 17 December. Overnight snow nearly scuppered it but in the end it was a Yeovil 'Blizzard' (Dominic that is) that helped to keep a clean sheet. Skivo commented afterwards that

*"We were on top defensively but didn't create much at the other end, but if I look at the bigger picture we've been beaten once in 10 league games, kept three clean sheets on the bounce and we're back to being hard to beat."*

It didn't seem to impress the Rochdale Board who immediately showed the door to their manager, Steve Eyre. Couldn't beat poor old Yeovil eh!

In all honesty that was not bad – beaten once in ten league games, could they keep it going over Christmas and the New Year?

Another one being shown the door in that week was the *Yeovil Express* newspaper, closing down after many years of reporting the 'glory years'. Many fans avidly read the reports from Express Chief Reporter, Steve Sowden. With his 'Keep the faith bruvvers' catchphrase he followed the Glovers all over the country in order to keep us up to date as the events as they unfolded. Thanks Steve. Now all we are left with is the *Western Gazette* to bring us the hard hitting investigative reports.

Christmas presents were handed out all round. Scarves, hats, duvet covers, three points to Charlton Athletic. That last one begrudgingly given by Yeovil who succumbed to a last minute strike in a five goal thriller against the league leaders. Unfortunately that put the Glovers back in the bottom four.

At least one *Green Room II* fan wrote in support:

*Unlucky  Yeovil they deserved a point against the league leaders ,unlucky skivo the team worked hard for you today ,gutted for you.* (yeoman)

## CHAPTER 4

# A SHAFT OF LIGHT

But whilst we waited for the arrival of Bournemouth in our New Year's Eve derby game others were turning their attention to some out of work guy living in Portishead.
Members of the forum posted:
*Yeovil now need a manager who can train his team to score goals as well as keep them out and at least know that strikers are for scoring goals, not painting the touchlines... Gary Johnson is the obvious choice for me, but maybe too obvious... perhaps it's totally fresh blood that we need... either way, SKIVO OUT!* (BucksGlover)

~~~~~~~~

*We'd better hurry up if we want GJ to come in, in what ever capacity, cos romour has it he could well end up at Rovers.* (Frankie)

~~~~~~~

*Why would we want Gary Johnson? He left us when we were struggling, you get highs and lows in the game and Johnson evidently just wanted the highs! I don't see Skivo running way, he's Yeovil through and through.*( YTFC0911)

~~~~~~~~~

*Gary Johnson did what every manager would do in that position... you get a better offer, you take the job... and GJ had been extremely loyal and successful for Yeovil until then and he is the reason we are in league one in the first place! He's had a rough few years and I can't see a better place for him to go and revive his career as I believe he is a wasted manager and I'll be shocked if he remains unemployed for long and Rovers would be making a very good move in appointing him should Buckle get the elbow...* (BucksGlover)

Well it all made logical sense surely, Gary lived in the Bristol area, Bristol Rovers were struggling at the wrong end of the League Two table. It would seem an obvious match. Well bugger logic. This is the 'Gas Heads' we're talking about here. He couldn't go there. It wouldn't be decent. They've got a wonderful manager in Paul Buckle ( supress laughter!) They were made for each other. Long may they sink together. Don't do it Gary!!

From what *Ciderspace* could make out in an item on 30th December Gary was not the only one possibly looking for a new home. Marek Stech, the young West Ham keeper we had for a month believed that West Ham wouldn't play him because they would have to make a stage payment to his old club Sparta Prague. Speaking to Czech Republic sports website *isport.blesk.cz* he hoped he might go out on loan to either Ipswich Town or Burnley for 6 months. *"Then I would have one year left on my West Ham deal and at such a situation you usually open talks over a new contract or move on."* Well as long as it's not to the Rovers, good luck.

Would Yeovil be able to finish the old year in style? Simple answer, No! Beaten 3-1 by Bournemouth *Ciderspace* in their match report (the details of which I shall not frighten you with) commented: 'The defeat sees the Glovers slip a place in the League One table, and with eight home defeats in 13 matches this season, it's not too hard to work out where Terry Skiverton's side need to improve. There have been too many poor performances at Huish Park this season. Just as the Glovers were spirited and skillful against Charlton Athletic on Boxing Day, they were poor against the Cherries. But the end result was the same on both occasions, and a few changes need to be made to the current squad if Yeovil are to climb out of this.'

Terry Skiverton spoke to Chris Spittles of BBC Somerset and said
"*We are freezing in home games but I truly believe we are going to get what we aim for. What we can't do is follow such a good performance against Charlton, when maybe we should have got something, and then fall flat (against Bournemouth). We gave two goals away and that left us with a mountain to climb. But we are in a better position than this time last season and I believe I have a better group of players this year.*"
Asked about the boos and verbal abuse that his players received at the end of the game, Terry replied:
 *It's not verbal abuse. It's just people who are frustrated. I don't consider that verbal abuse, because what I said at half time was a lot worse than what they were saying. That was verbal abuse! (laughs) I know most of the supporters. I've been here long enough. You've got to take it on the chin. I've had the pats on the back at this football club. We're going through a tough time. We know that.*
*But one thing we do know, and I want the supporters to know, is that we're working as hard as we can. I sat down with the board this week, and I've put across my targets of players that I want to bring in, to help the squad get to where we've got to get to. They've been quite accommodating with that. So we'll see in these next coming weeks who we bring in. But there's a couple of*

*positions that I'm really looking for, that will definitely strengthen us in the right areas.*

*Green RoomII* pundits were furiously hitting the keypads:
*Can we not get a manager in on loan as we are a small club no money no pasties nothing going for us at all.* (Rolfo)

~~~~~~~~~~

*Look forward to seeing Accrington Stanley next season.....(Swat)*

~~~~~~~~~

*And Forest Green the year after, if Skivo stays in charge.* (yeoviljohn)

~~~~~~~~~~

*People say Skivo should go – well maybe he should but frankly I think most of that team should donate their match fees to a local charity. I didn't boo them at the end, I merely left, disappointed. I remember GJ looked for 3 things in a player, good technique, physical fitness and a quickness of thought. Today we looked predictable, slow of thought and physically unfit.* (Oracle)

There was no time to cry over the spilt milk as yet another local derby was looming on 2nd January 2012 – Exeter City away. This was a chance to start the New Year in the right manner. Well nearly! 1-1 was the final score which kept Yeovil in the relegation zone. But there was good news. Because of the F.A. Cup 3rd Round we had no game on the following Saturday. Also bad news, the next game would be Sheffield United away.

At least we could take a breather and prepare ourselves for the downward run, sorry poor choice of phrase, to the end of the season. I could have put the upward run down to the end of the season but it wouldn't have made a lot of sense. Did Skivo know his ups from his downs by this time? It must have seemed a very lonely position that he occupied as manager. Ok he had Nathan and Daren to consult with but at the end of the day the buck stopped with him. Would he be able to turn the season around as he had done the year before? All would be revealed.

With the Sheffield United game some eight whole days away fans could relax, take it easy, finish the Christmas turkey and try on those lucky Yeovil socks they had from Granny. With nothing to write about I thought I could express this with a blank page and give us all a break.

However those clever guys at *Ciderspace* had not taken their eye of the ball and on 4th January they reported: 'Former Yeovil Town manager Gary Johnson has thrown out a fairly major hint that he is willing to consider taking over the managerial reins at Bristol Rovers. The Fulham-born 56 year old appeared on both *BBC Points West* and *BBC Bristol* yesterday, merely hours after the League Two strugglers had fired Paul Buckle after just 24 League games in charge at the Memorial Stadium.'

Speaking to *BBC Points West*, Johnson described himself as a 'West Country' man (in a broad cockney accent, of course!) drawing attention to the fact that despite having taken jobs with Peterborough United and Northampton Town since leaving Bristol City, he still owns an apartment in Bristol. Out of work since being fired by the Cobblers in November, he appears not to like Daytime TV too much, and refused to deny interest in the position:
"*You don't rule anything out. I class myself as a West Country person and this is where I enjoyed all my football. Of course I'm interested in everything that comes up. I want to get back into management. I can't stand sitting at home and watching (TV programme) Loose Women, it's driving me up the wall.*"

Since Rovers sacked Paul Trollope in December 2010, they had rattled up a conveyor belt of managers, with Darren Patterson (caretaker), Dave Penney, Stuart Campbell, Paul Buckle and Shaun North (caretaker, just appointed) all trying their luck but invariably failing. Having been relegated from League One last season, they now languished in 19th place in League Two, but Johnson believed that whoever was capable of turning them around would be managing a big club:
"*It's going to be a decent job for somebody. It's a big club with a great fan base and lots of potential. They've got to find someone who can turn it round quickly and get Rovers back up that table.*"
*Ciderspace* commented: 'There have been little whispers on the rumour mill of Johnson returning to Huish Park, in some capacity, on and off since he left Sixfields, however there's no doubt that a front line management position is going to appeal to him, particularly one on his own doorstep.'

Many a heart must have slumped when this item got a general airing in the Yeovil area. There was much pulling apart of the phraseology that Gary had used. Was this really a 'major hint' or was it someone distancing himself from the position? Those that are really interested in a post say something like "Well I haven't been approached yet but if I was I would certainly give it serious consideration. I am flattered to be linked with this job at such an ambitious club" He didn't say that. He says "It's going to be a decent job for somebody" A bit of distance don't you think? I know, I know, we were all clutching at straws. Truth was it all looked inevitable. Rovers were poised to whisk him away.

It was business as usual at Huish Park for Skivo. As the transfer window had opened up a couple of players were moving on, a couple of loan players were not coming back and Terry had a couple of irons in the fire:

*"We have got decisions to make as a football club and I have got to make sure that I am making the right ones and that the players I bring in are of an equal quality or even better. I have got my eye on a few and we will see who we bring in over the next 20 or so days as there are some really exciting names. I need to make sure we bring the right ones in."*

6th January is of course 12th Night. While we sang the final verses of 'The Twelve Days of Christmas' including wishing for 12 Home End Drummers Drumming and 6 Geese a laying (preferably Golden Eggs to buy a striker) , not a few were secretly praying for our own 'Cockney Sparrow' to be up our Wurzel tree!'.

As the hours ticked by and day followed night into the 7th January 2012 those of a twitchy nature might have had an extra tick when news came from Brizzle that the Rovers were about to announce their new manager. In a nano second the name Mark McGhee fluttered over the airwaves and South Somerset breathed a sigh of relief. No mistake then, Johnson doesn't sound anything like McGhee. We heard it right – Rovers had missed a trick.
But then, if Mr Johnson wasn't going to the Gas Heads.....where???
Then like a shooting star and Halley's Comet all rolled into one, the night sky lit up as BBC Somerset's Chris Spittles suggested that  Gary Johnson was in talks with Yeovil Town about a possible role at the club. The BBC local sports editor, Geoff Twentyman went further and stated that he expected Johnson to be lined up as first team manager. They suggested that all would become clearer next week. Clearer next week!! The Northern Lights and the Midnight Sun were glaring down and all was bright and clear. Gary Johnson was coming home!!!

The *Green Room II* faithful were up and away:
*This is a masterstroke if this appointment goes ahead, as GJ will bring the pride back to Somerset and the club which is at rock bottom imho at the moment.*
*A week ago i was feeling sick of the thought that rovers who i detest as a club could possibly have GJ as their manager ,unbelievable that a week later he could be walking back into Huish Park.*
*Maybe there is a football god looking down on little old Yeovil Town FC.*(sedgy)

~~~~~~~~~~

*we may have to go down with GJ at the helm to rebuild but if there is someone who really understands YTFC it is GJ and he is a manager who pulls it all together and inspires fans to get behind him, he will be the boss of that dressing room and we badly need that right now, a leader.* (kmglover)

~~~~~~~~

*I for one is very pleased that Gary Johnson could be coming back to manage us but please can people stop putting him up on a pedestal  so soon and treating him as the messiah as he is not the messiah he is just a very good manager who can save our club from the hell of non- league football again.* (glover-tom)

~~~~~~~~

*He's not the Messiah - just a..... (altogether now!)* (unspeakable cad)

~~~~~~~~~

*Very naughty boy.....* (Ytfc117)

*Ciderspace* were straight onto it, announcing every step that was being made, from time of the Press Conference at Huish Park to news that Terry Skiverton was likely to be made Assistant Manager. Without fanfares and whistles they said: 'Yeovil Town have this afternoon formally welcomed back Gary Johnson as their new first team manager this afternoon. In what has been one of the worst kept secrets of the past two days, 'Sir Gary' has completed a full circle started when he left the club in September 2005, taking him via Bristol City, Peterborough United and Northampton Town, and now back to Huish Park.
Gary takes up the reins, with Terry Skiverton becoming his assistant manager, having relinquished a role he had held since February 2009. He took charge for 144 matches, clocking up 38 wins, 41 draws and 65 defeats during his time in the hot seat.

Yeovil Town's new manager Gary Johnson has said that he is willing to retain Nathan Jones and Darren Way as part of the coaching staff, if all parties involved can reach agreement...... one of the unanswered questions of the management changes has been where that leaves Jones and Way in the club's set-up.

Speaking during this afternoon's press conference, Johnson believed that the pair had 'opportunities' to stay with the club, but did not reveal what their job titles would be:

*"They certainly have the opportunity to remain in posts. Obviously I've only been here this morning, and I've been out and we've been doing a bit of work with the lads in preparation for the game tomorrow. But yes, they're also great stalwarts of the club - Nathan (Jones) and Darren (Way) - and we'd love to keep them around."*

Reports from the press who were at the session suggested that Gary plans to meet with the board later in the week to make certain proposals regarding the management structure, which may explain why Jones and Way have yet to have any new job titles revealed. Johnson said it was important that both him and Skiverton knew both parties well:

*"Terry (Skiverton) has been working with them and he trusts them. I've known them from previous years. So it's a perfect scenario. All four of us love the club. We all helped to get the club where it is now, so we haven't suddenly jumped into somebody else's success, and we'd like to take it further."'*

Those of you who fully understand 'Twitter' and all its ramifications will be delighted to know that Gary Johnson appeared at No.9 in the UK trends on 9th January. People couldn't stop tweeting about the wonderful news. Oh and at No. 8 was Peppa Pig. Thought you'd like to know.

A contributor to 'Taff's Blog' on *Ciderspace* wrote:

*A sense of sadness for Skivo, and a sense of hope that GJ will keep us in League One. The obvious reality is that nothing is certain, Johnson returns at the lowest ebb in his managerial carer to less ambitious and optimistic circumstances than those he rejected years before, but there is no doubt the prospect of staying up, better attendances, and the general mood, have all received a boost.*

*Welcome back and good luck, Gary, and also a sincere thank you and good luck to Skivo whatever he does from this point - whether involved with the club or not - and naturally the same for Nathan Jones and Darren Way, as we also await a decision on their futures at the club. .*

*Whatever happens, through his playing career and his impact on this club through his commitment and loyalty, Terry Skiverton has also walked on Huish Park water and also has his place in Yeovil history cast in stone. And will command an everlasting and deserved respect and admiration of the highest standard, that at any club, only a few ever achieve.*

I said at the beginning that the roots of a love affair can go back quite a long way and may take many a twist and turn before blossoming . What would have happened if we had stuck it out for another ten minutes at Fleetwood and won 2-0. We would have been able to have a tilt at Blackpool in Round 3. What if we had won that one??? Who knows. We might have drawn someone mega and become the darlings of all underdogs across the land.  If we had just picked up a point or three over the Christmas and New Year period would we, the fans have been baying for a change at the top?  Would the Board have felt the need to replace the man they had so recently publicly supported? Probably not.  We are after all a fickle bunch, as are all football supporters and Board members. We blow hot and cold on a daily basis depending on a goal scored, or one conceded. A good result, or a poor run. A Supermarket or a Social Club!

Of course we, here at Yeovil, are green and white to the core, even the ones who have chosen to stay away this season.  But back to what if? If things had gone just slightly differently would Gary Johnson have even be on our radar? Would the Board have approached him? Why would they have bothered? Why rock the ship? Perhaps Gary Johnson might have found himself on the daily commute from Portishead to the Memorial Ground and given the Gas a leg up in League 2.  For all the above thank goodness 'the what ifs' didn't happen. It was written in the stars after all that the prodigal son, 'Sir' Gary Johnson would return.

Well there it is, that's what happened. For good or bad, time would tell. This book so far has not exactly been filled with sunshine, well not until the last few pages anyway.  What has been written has not been done with any motive other than to set the scene of what was to come. A history book and this is what it is, needs to deal with the facts of the time and the opinions and perceptions of those who were involved and interested as the events unfolded.  All of us who have been connected with Yeovil Town in whatever capacity have helped to shape the continuing story of our famous little old club. From the Chairman and owner, the members of the Board, the management team, players, ours and loanees, the fans, those that attend Huish Park, those that for one reason or another only attended away games and those fans who for all various reasons had not been watching any of the live games but continued their interest by watching out for the results at 5.00pm on a Saturday.

The history of the Club builds in layers, each passing season usually falls neatly into being a chapter of the story. However this time it seemed that one chapter was closing half way through the season and another new chapter was just about to begin. It felt like we were having two mini seasons. The one that had ended had brought about  games played 23,wins 4,draw8 defeats 11, final placing 22nd. Luckily for us in these circumstances it didn't  mean relegation Our second mini season, which was to begin at Bramall Lane on Tuesday gave us 22 games to start anew and try and catch a few of the teams above us. Interesting times ahead.

Before we get back to the sharp end of the business and all the on field activity, it would only be right and proper to thank Terry Skiverton for the tremendous efforts that he has put in on behalf of Yeovil Town. As a player it is only necessary to say 'Legend'. A Yeovil Town hero for ever. Total respect. Management is a totally different kettle of fish and no seasoned professional football player can know at the start of this new career whether he will be able to make the grade. Yes he will have spent years in the company of various managers, learning from their skills, their weaknesses, their successes and failures but when that day comes and he is the gaffer, what then.  That day came for Terry probably sooner than he expected and he naturally grabbed it with both hands.

Given the task of keeping Yeovil at the highest level that had been achieved in more than 100 years, on probably one of the smallest playing budgets in the league, he did exactly what it said on the tin. Despite being the bookies favourite to go down in each of his three years in charge, he defied the odds and kept us up. Yes, the pressure was certainly on this 2011/12 season, results had not run kindly, the F.A. Cup was a disaster, but Terry stuck to the task and was always positive about the job he had to do. It was obvious that he loved being the manager and it could not have been easy to be told that someone was going to be brought in to do his job and he would be offered an assisting role.

Later on Gary Johnson threw some light on the situation when he spoke in interview with Graham Nickless:*"In football you have to make really important decisions for yourself and your family and Terry must have had a real difficult predicament in his head. I sat down with him for four or five hours in a hotel and convinced him that I would still make him feel like he was co-manager. Because he trusted me from his playing days he knew he had to let it go."*

It could only have worked between these two. There was obviously a special chemistry between them. It took a big man to step back from the number one position and become a subordinate. It could be argued that any job in these days is worth having, with the mortgage to pay and the kids to feed but Terry could have walked away and would probably have picked up another managerial position, maybe at a lower level, but surely somewhere pretty swiftly. But what seemed to stand out is that he was Yeovil through and through and he took the decision because it was in the interest of the Club. Some months later Gary Johnson was to reveal that he was not prepared to take the job unless Terry Skiverton was there by his side. Thank you Terry.

There also has to be a thank you here to Chairman John Fry. Thank you for bringing Gary Johnson to Huish Park first time round and now a huge thank you for doing it again. Even if you do nothing else in your term as Chairman you will long be remembered for those two masterstrokes.

OK so the season starts here and there is a bit of catch up to do. First off is that long journey north to Sheffield. Even before Gary and the lads are on the coach eating up the motorway miles, the Chairman, John Fry gave out a strong warning. Speaking to BBC Somerset he said: *"There's no point in me standing here telling you that we're going to dig out money, and so forth and so on.......... We've got limited resources. Gary knows what he is having to deal with. Let him see what the squad is like, let's see what the size of this problem is, and we'll answer it."* It has to come through the gates and you have to earn it. The club has during the last three years lost about a million pounds on its gate receipts. The gates have gone down from about four-and-a-half (thousand) down to three-and-a-half (thousand). It's about whether

*Gary can bring the crowds back and produce more income. You can't spend more than what you've got. If you do, then you go broke."*

Right here is the task Gary, get a successful team together that will cost no more than a few Mars bars and then go out and sell tickets for the stands in your spare time. Wow we knew he was good but this!! Obviously the Chairman won't have sprung this news on GJ and by agreeing to whatever contract he has signed he is fully prepared to work within the restraints that are put before him. We all know the brand and philosophy in Gary's style. Attack and score one more than them. It is what we have loved in the past. Could he do it again? Even if he could would it bring back those missing punters to Huish Park. We all knew of long time season ticket holders who had not renewed and went on to do other things on a Saturday afternoon. It could be a struggle to entice them back. But if anyone could Gary could. Having said that it would be nice to think that perhaps others at the Club might also step up to the mark and give him a hand.

Probably with the Chairman's words "Let him see what the squad is like, let's see what the size of the problem is" still in his head he, like the hardy 175 fans who travelled to chilly Sheffield saw that the squad was poor and the size of the problem was huge. A 4-0 walloping by a promotion chasing United showed up many of the frailties in the Yeovil team. Speaking to the press afterwards he said:

*"Nobody thought it was going to be easy. This wouldn't have been the game I'd have chosen for my first game back but in a way it's showed me sort of what I already knew and that the group at this moment in time has to change for us to be competitive. I don't think anybody's ever been sacked after a day so I think I'm all right but there are some players there who are okay and we can work with but there are some that are not. We've just got to work very hard in the next couple of weeks with no days off and all that sort of thing." ......We mustn't go out of this league with a whimper or with players that are not quite up for it. We've got to see that quickly and turn it round."*

The new broom began to sweep. Next day the first new arrival was announced, Joe Edwards, defender, on loan from Bristol City. One player who said he definitely would not be coming to Huish Park was Lee

Johnson. It seems that he has had enough of playing under his Dad. Fair enough.

Shortly after the first departures began. Loan players were shipped out and one of our own, Paul Wootton, was show the door and given a map back to Plymouth. Things were happening in a whirlwind. The fans were delighted. , Cameras! Action! This was like a Hollywood movie. Hero returns from the wilderness and catapults Village Pub Team into the Premiership, watched at first by two men and a dog but eventually by full houses in a new Stadium (complete with Social Club)

The buzz around the town was palpable. Excitement was growing by the minute as the clock ticked by to Saturday afternoon and the visit of Tranmere Rovers.

The *Green Room II* was being inundated with posts from fans supporting the appointment of Gary, also supporting the valiant efforts of Skivo. All were keen to be at Huish Park for the great return. New lyrics to a favourite song were proposed:
*I JUST CAN'T WAIT TILL SATURDAY!*                    *Put on yer hats, Wave yer flags grab yer shirts.......*
*'HE'S COMING HOME...HE'S COMING HOME...HE'S COOMMMING!*
*JOHNSONS COMING HOME!*
*YEOVIL ON HIS SHIRT..*
*GREEN AND WHITE ARE FIGHTING...*
*7 YEARS OF HURT..*
*NOW WE'RE BACK UNITED...*
*HE'S COMING HOME....HE'S COMING HOME.'* (Judd)

~~~~~~~~~~
*What else can we do to make it unique and special and intimidating? I mean apart from numbers and flags?*
*All bring a scarf to twirl? Just something!!!!* (Ytfc117)

A midfield loan player was soon drafted in from Tottenham Hotspur, Dean Parrett. Those that knew the name were more than happy.

A rumour ran around that Terry Skiverton might have been offered the Manger's job at Stevenage. A certain Mr Graham Westley presently occupied the hot seat but it was widely believed that he was about to take over Preston North End. Like many a rumour it was only partially true. Skivo did not go but Westley did. Lucky old Preston!

The stage was set, the script was written, all that was required was for everyone to play their part. Gary took the adulation from the crowd, the new loanee, Joe Edwards scored a debut goal and then Andy Williams scored the winner in the 94th minute. 4,083 fans, minus a few Tranmere, went home more than satisfied. 2-1 the final score, three points in the bag and thank you very much.

In the following week there were more comings and goings. A new goalkeeper, Sam Walker, on loan until the end of the season and Kelly Youga from Bristol City. In the other direction Max Ehmer was going back home to QPR

Bury away came next. Disappointment with a 3-2 defeat showed that we shouldn't get too carried away. There would be a lot of work to be done to get Yeovil to safety by the end of the season.

28th January. Preston North End at home. 2-1 to the Glovers. A passionate encounter, ending with one sent off for each side. But passion is what we wanted from a Yeovil Team. We were glad to see it back. (Crowd 4245)

30 January: Bournemouth splash the cash with £800,000 on Crawley's Matt Tubbs. Yes he's the one that played for Salisbury a while ago.

On the *Green RoomII* forum supporters were chatting:

*In the wake of AFC Bournemouth spending 800k on Matt Tubbs from Crawley, I think I am, for once, glad we are not spending this sort of money on Strikers in lower leagues. Bournemouth are a very similar club to Yeovil, which should mean we have similar ambitions. But this is not the case. Is it fair to say that they are over ambitious for where they are and we are completely under ambitious (I'm not sure if that is the correct term)? Part of me would love to see us spend some money on decent players, but then the other is cautious and would not want to over spend.*

*Would you rather be taking the risk of AFC Bournemouth big budget busting buys, on the premise that its promotion or bust? Or would you scrimp, save and not take a risk in the likes of Yeovil?*

*It's a question I have been thinking about all day and I cannot decide.* ( Like-a- glove)

~~~~~~~~~

*Bmuff have now had an improved offer accepted by Swindon for Matt Ritchie, the last offer was 500k!!!!* (PETERSANDALL)

In anticipation of our own mega dip into the transfer market, fans were writing:

*Think we could be in for an exciting day tomorrow* (NBGlover)

~~~~~~~

*Only if you aren't expecting anything from Huish.....*(Dazz)

~~~~~~~~

*Hope you have a good day at Bristol Zoo* (glover-tom)

No great expectations there then.

## CHAPTER 5

# SAFETY FIRST

The transfer market window closed on 31st January without Yeovil doing any further business. The loan market would soon open and we could see further movement then. However, we managed to sign up former Sheffield Wednesday defender, Richard Hinds, who was just out of contract. Hinds would be necessary to fill in for Paul Huntingdon, sent off against Preston and now serving a lengthy ban.

I could, I guess give you every detail of all of the remaining game of the season, every interview that Gary gave and a sprinkling of fans views and opinions. The book you would now be reading would be the size of 'War and Peace' and just about as boring. Let's face it the season was memorable for only two reasons. One, the return of Gary Johnson and two, we kept our League One status.

Let's stick with that earlier Hollywood movie theme. We now have it all on DVD, so push the fast forward button and we will shoot on towards the end of the season, pausing only to chuck in the odd snippet of information as we go.  Naturally feel free to pause, go out and make a coffee and think about how you were feeling as the results piled up and safety became assured. Come back refreshed, ready to continue our journey down memory lane.

 4 February :  Weather forecast – Ice and Snow. No problem for Hillsborough. Under soil heating ensured the game went ahead. Pity – Sheffield Wednesday 2 -1 Yeovil.

7 February and the Club submitted their formal Retail Planning Application to the South Somerset District Council.  John Fry says if plan 'A' is rejected, there is no plan 'B'!! Plan 'A' it is then.

Another vacancy arises and fans are straight on to it:

*Capello resigns, Skivo in talks with F.A.* (PETESANDALL)

~~~~~~~

*As long as the FA is clear that GJ is TAKEN!* (Unspeakable cad)

12 February: Shock, horror, Trevor Kettle is announced as Referee for the next game.

*Arguably one of the most vital games this season against Wycombe Tuesday - a win is a must for both teams...*
*and it had to be THAT day, that bloody Kettle is the man in the middle... can we expect much more than a draw and some decisions that cost us the game and Gary Johnson fined £2,500 for his post-match interview??*(Bucks Glover)
~~~~~~~
*To be honest Kettle is one of the worst refs that I have ever seen in all my years as a Yeovil supporter.*(cuzzie)
~~~~~~~
*ONE of the worst?? Surely there is no one worse.* (swat)

15 February: Wycombe Wanderers 2 – 3 Yeovil. A couple of goals from our star striker, Andy Williams.

League 1 side Huddersfield sacked manager Lee Clark despite sitting in a healthy playoff position in fourth spot. Tough at the top.

17 February: Championship club Portsmouth went into administration for the second time. A club known to grossly overspend had been at it again. £1.9 million owed to just the taxman. Overall figure of debt thought to be £138.6 million.  At least a ten point deduction should see them visiting Huish Park next time round (If it turned out that we remained in League 1.)

18 February: Yeovil 3 – 2 Colchester United. Another goal from Andy Williams!  And the first senior goal for new boy Lawson D'Ath. Gary said of it: *Everyone always remembers their first senior goal. I think that was his family over there that he ran into. They can't book him for running into the crowd, cos that was his family! I don't think it counts!"*

Yeovil lay in 18th place with the likes of Walsall, Scunthorpe and Rochdale close behind .( Crowd:3442)

On the same afternoon Notts County relieved 'Mad Dog' Martin Allen of his duties. They lay in 11th position but with a track record of sacking 6 managers in just over two years I guess it was no great surprise.

22/23 February. Three more players sign up. Two on month's loans – Middlesbrough's Jonathan Franks and Jonathan Grounds and former Chelsea midfielder, Michael Woods, on non-contract terms.

25th February: Carlisle 3 – 2 Yeovil. 120 brave souls made the long, long trek. Oh and a lad by the name of Patrick Madden was playing for Carlisle. Useless apparently.

28 February: Both Brympton Parish Council and Yeovil Town Council gave the thumbs down to the Retail project. Amongst Brympton's concerns were *'The lack of information on how the holding company will transfer the funds raised to the Football Club.'* Interesting! More than a few fans had similar concerns.

The Town Council in their recommendation for refusal, sited as one of the grounds: *'It will have an adverse effect upon the well-being of Yeovil Town Centre.'*                              Some of the Town Councillors were quoted in the *Western Gazette* as saying that it would "*drag the heart out of the town*" and                              "*That is horrendous. It is going to cause diabolical mayhem. It is totally rubbish*". Not looking good then.

In response Chairman, John Fry said:                              "*We were extremely surprised and disappointed with the views. However, the club remains committed and determined to work constructively with South Somerset District Council and all other parties to secure a successful outcome to our development proposals. These proposals are vital for the future of the football club, our supporters and the wider community*."

3 March: Yeovil 2 – 1 Brentford (Why does that score sound familiar?) Andy Williams with both goals. (Crowd 3930)

5 March: Tranmere Rovers seem to want to try the 'return of the Manager' trick. Out goes Les Parry and returning for his fourth spell is Ronnie Moore. Also show the door is Hereford's manager, Jamie Pitman. You were always too good for the Bulls Jamie.

7 March. Away at Franchise United in the Mk stadium. Pure joy!! MK Dons 0 -1 Yeovil Town. A super Gav goal. The win put us 5 points clear of the drop zone, staying in 17th place. 2nd in the table on current form.

This Gary Johnson bloke's not half bad!

When asked by a reporter how it felt to have won, Gary replied: *"You're the educated one - you find some words, because I can't! I'm so proud - and that's all I can say. They hung on in there. They were up against 13 or 14 players; 11 in white and three in black! But the lads hung on in there and they deserved the result."*

From the forum: *We came, we saw, we robbed them blind* .(HHH)

10 March: Oldham Athletic 1 – 2 Yeovil Town. This time both Williams' got on the score sheet.

13 March Yeovil 2 – 2 Scunthorpe United. It was Super Gav again. I wouldn't mind some of what he was on at the time. (Crowd 3767)

Chairman John Fry as part of the live broadcast of the match by BBC Somerset spoke to Chris Spittles:
*"Our aim is to go to the upper end of the table and try to get into the Championship. What we have to do is build the stadium facilities to that standard. The stadium is incomplete.*
*After 20 years it's becoming derelict. The site itself is derelict. The astro-pitch is finished with. The top pitch is not fit for purpose, and the car parks need improving and the highways etc. We're not doing this just to get a food store and increase money for the hell of it. We're doing this for the future and the security of the football club."*

Hang on there a minute did he say *"try and get into the Championship".* This is naked ambition and we love it. Say it again, go on, please.

14 March: To support the Club's efforts in bringing the food store to Huish Park Gary made a DVD requesting that supporters should lobby the Council and support the Club. The way things look though, this DVD could be sharing a dusty shelf with the one entitled 'Greatest Throw Ins – 2009'. It seems that for the application to have a snowball's chance in Hell, the Club have to identify areas for replacement training pitches. Do we have

any? If this is to be a game of two halves then it is going to take a special half time team talk from someone like Gary to get Yeovil in with a chance of turning it around.

17 March: Yeovil 2 – 1 Walsall. Andy Williams scored them both. Thoughts were that wouldn't it be great if we could start to build a team around this lad for next season. 46 points and 12th. They were nearly there.(Crowd 3705)

20 March: Always a big ask at high flying Charlton – Charlton 3 – 0 Yeovil.

24 March: Not sure that we saw this one coming after recent results but Yeovil 0-1 Hartlepool. The Monkey Hangers top supporter, Jeff Stelling on Gillette Soccer Saturday will have loved this one.

25 March: Yeovil's next opponents, AFC Bournemouth sack their manager, Lee Bradbury. Paul Groves and Shaun Brooks take over until the end of the season. What effect would that have on the next game?

30 March: Gary Johnson speaking to BBC Somerset pledged that the club would try their hardest to keep their star players. With sixteen players out of contract in a few games time he said:
*"Certainly with the ones who have been playing regularly, we'll be looking to talk to them, and try to keep for this club. But there's lots of other things out there for them; lots of other clubs, lots of other agents. So we'll have to wait and see. But all we can do is try our hardest to keep them."*

He added that in his opinion three points should secure League 1 status for next season. Bournemouth on Saturday would be a nice time to get them.

31March: Wishful thinking is not always enough. Just the one point for the Glovers in a 0 – 0 draw with AFC Bournemouth.

2 April: The Club announced an operating profit of £21,000 for the year 2010/11. Exactly the same as the year before. When you look around at the debts that many clubs are racking up that's not bad.

7 April: The magic 50 points were reached as Yeovil dispatched relegation bound Rochdale 3-1. After the other results of the day it

looked very much like Chesterfield, Exeter City and Wycombe Wanderers would be following them down.

Gary said afterwards:
*"The results we have been getting since I came back to Somerset have been really encouraging. I have pointed out to the lads that if recent form had been spread over the season, we would not be far from the play-offs."*

14April: Worst home defeat since 1958! Yeovil 0 – 6 Stevenage. Not quite play-off form but let's put it into perspective. In 1901 we got beat 15-0 by Devizes Some good news; Yeovil Town Ladies were presented with the League Trophy, having won the South West Combination League title.

With the sixteen lads out of contract in a few weeks, Gary Johnson had this to say after the mauling:

*"They could not have even spoken to me let along talk to me about new deals and on Monday and Tuesday nobody was getting new contracts. That was not the right time, or if it had been I would have been in a very strong position, I would have thought. But in all seriousness, we are going to do it before the end of this week. I want to go on my holidays with at least a few pencilled in. If it is the boys already at the club they will sign a contract before they leave for the summer, hopefully, and if it not those boys I will try to tie up or pencil in a few that are not at the club already."*

21 April: Safety at last. Leyton Orient 2 – 2 Yeovil. We were staying Up!

28th April: Final home game of the season. Yeovil 3 – 2 Chesterfield. There was a minute's applause for the passing of Dave Platt at the age of 55 years. Dave played for Yeovil Town between 1978 -1985 and scored 61 goals. R.I.P.

Andy Williams scored again and Chesterfield were relegated. Gary Johnson stayed late that evening at Huish Park as he shook just about every supporter's hand. (Crowd 4563)

Fans were in a reflective mood as minds began to turn to next season:
*I as almost everyone else was surprised and very pleased about Jonno senior's return to YTFC, a masterstroke or lucky chance I don't care but now with safety confirmed we can now review GJs return. Remember the early doubts about managers returns and will it work out, well at present I think*

*we can safely say yes (to date). Some ups and downs but I believe the magic has returned to HP. Whether or not we keep some or all of our stars this summer I am really excited about the prospect of next season with GJ at the helm.* (Judd)

~~~~~~~~ *The achievement of turning a team that was in a relegation spot and was playing truly awful football under Skivo to a team that will finish in 15th/16th is pretty da-mn good.*

*As a spectator it is the style of football that has been so refreshing after 2/3 years of generally defensive minded 10 men behind the ball tactics to if were 1-0 up lets carry on attacking to make it 2-0.*
*We have played a lot more on the ground and as today some of the moves and passing has been great to watch.*
*Next season as long as we stay up not too bothered about finishing position as long as we play attractive attack minded football.* (valetta baby)

29 April: *Ciderspace* reported that: 'Yeovil Town manager Gary Johnson has claimed that the club have given the 'biggest' contract offer they have ever made to a player in their efforts to keep their leading goalscorer beyond the summer. Striker Andy Williams netted his 17th goal of the season in yesterday's 3-2 win over Chesterfield, but will be entitled to leave the club on a free transfer with his two year contract expiring at the end of the season.'

Speaking after the game, Gary admitted to *BBC Somerset* that after such a prolific season that the 25 year old was bound to get offers from other clubs. But he felt that the Glovers had put in a strong offer to persuade him to stay:
*"Everybody has an opportunity at some point to do something after a decent season. I think everybody appreciates where they were and what that club did for them. But we're not going to be able to entice him through sentiment. Andy has been made probably the biggest offer this club has ever made to somebody, and it's on his table now.*
*We made that offer to him early, and it will be up to him. He's obviously got to look at his options as that's the professional thing to do. I hope he stays - of course I do, because I think we are going to be competing next year and it would be nice if we have got him with us, rather than not with us."*

2 May: Just when you thought that football was all about money, greed and debt, 299 Huddersfield supporters set off from Huish Park to bike ride the 250 miles back to their ground in time to host Yeovil in the final match of the season They planned a short detour to lay flowers in memory of the LFC supporters who lost their lives in the Hillsborough disaster. The Challenge was in aid of the Yorkshire Air Ambulance.

*Green Room II* fans warmed to the idea and donations flooded in together with good wishes:
*This is such a worthy cause, good luck to you all & have a safe journey.*(Lorraine)

~~~~~~~~~~

*Good luck, good saddle and good pants!* (GreenDome)

~~~~~~~~~

*Good luck guys..... I'm driving up and that seems a long enough trip so I have no idea how you're cycling it! It's a great cause though so all the best in your efforts.* (Blackthorn Stand)

5 May: Huddersfield Town 2 – 0 Yeovil Town. Huddersfield marched on to the Play-Offs while we have eyes only for next season. All over then, safety in 17th place in the league. And immediately the first of the building blocks for next season's campaign is laid. Speaking to the BBC Gary Johnson announced Ed Upson's decision to sign for two years
*"The good news is that one of them already this morning - Ed Upson - has told us that he will be signing, so he'll be certainly signing early on Tuesday. He's committed himself to us for the next two years, which is fantastic as I think he'll only get better, and since I've been here he's been a fantastic player, a great person and a real pro. So he's a good one to get the old domino effect started."*
Just the I's to dot and the T's to cross and we were done with 2011/12.

Leaving us in an upward direction were Charlton Athletic (Champions), Sheffield Wednesday and one from Sheffield United, Huddersfield Town, MK Dons and Stevenage through the Play-Offs. Going in the other direction were Wycombe Wanderers, Chesterfield, Exeter City and Rochdale.

Joining us from the Championship would be Doncaster Rovers, Portsmouth and Coventry City and from League Two, Swindle Town, Shrewsbury Town  and Crawley Town, with one from either Southend United, Torquay United, Cheltenham Town and Crewe Alexandra.

## CHAPTER 6

# TOPLESS

Now we could all sit back, enjoy the Play-Off's, twiddle our fingers and look forward to the announcement of the new Fixture List. Lazy Saturday afternoons on the sun lounger, sipping an ice cold beer, not a care in the world. Apart that is from two things. One, it started to rain from the beginning of May and never stopped all summer. The second worry, well at least for some sixty two posters on *Green Room II* was the status of Andy Williams. Would he sign, would he walk. Who would snatch him up. Would he go Up North to Rotherham or stay in the South:
*To Swindle* (rock and roll)

~~~~~~~

*Not a chance* (gatez4000)

~~~~~~~

*I'd of lost most respect for him if he makes a sideways move to someone like them.*(ToggsYTFC)

~~~~~~~

*If true and he has that little ambition, then good riddance.*(Dazz)

~~~~~~~

*Trouble is.... Money talks with such short careers. There can't be many clubs in the football league offering less than YTFC* (rock and roll)

~~~~~~~

*After looking at it, I don't think losing A Williams will be a big loss, over the last 5 years I think he has scored somewhere in the region of 34 goals which isn't a great record at all. As the previous poster said, this season he has hit a purple patch and even then he has been hit and miss in games. There's nothing to say next season he won't even make double figures. I've got complete trust in GJ to bring in the right players and I really do think we will be in the top 10 next season.* (theoneandonly)

~~~~~~~

*I have my money on him being the player to unveil next seasons kit on Thursday, combined with the news that he has signed a new contract . Probably not but I can dream....* (Southsea Green)

See what happens when people are forced to stay indoors and tap on their keyboards!

News kept rolling in. The good -Super Gav and Luke Ayling signed for another season. The bad- Dr.Tony Simmonds, Yeovil Town's Club doctor for approximately 35 years passed away having battled against cancer for some time.  Terry Skiverton said:
*"So sad to hear the loss of Doc Simmonds. Wise, funny, caring, professional and a good friend to me when things ever got tough. The whole community will miss him."*

An important fixture, postponed due to a waterlogged pitch in January was played on 13 May. The much coveted Adam Stansfield Memorial Trophy was played out between Yeovil and Exeter supporters, with Exeter coming out on top for the first time in four attempts. Most importantly, the match raised the sum of £177 towards the Adam Stansfield Foundation. Well done to all who were involved.

The following day, 14 May came the news that many were dreading. *Ciderspace* reported: 'Yeovil Town have confirmed that four of last season's squad have left the club after failing to accept contract offers at Huish Park. Striker Andy Williams and midfielder Dominic Blizzard have failed to agree terms at the club, whilst Middlesbrough loan duo Jonathan Grounds and Jonathan Franks have also turned down a chance to join the club permanently.'

Fortunately one of those was a mix up in communication and he did sign. No it wasn't Andy Williams but Dominic Blizzard. Williams was defiantly off to pastures new. But where?

And still the rain continued to fall. Just as well there were new Home and Away kits to talk about on *Green Room II:*

*I really like them! Look really smart!* (YTFC0911)

~~~~~~~

*Agreed. Hope the 'bright yellow' they mention isn't the same as we had this year though. I like the way the away one looks on the OS but I'm not keen on another luminous away kit!* (CapitalGreen)

~~~~~~~

*Personally not a fan, would prefer full green as it just looks a messy to me. Hope the away is a nice yellow and not too bright, looks like a bumble bee! Good that the majority appear happy as it's the majority that the club need to buy it, unfortunately on first impressions it'll be another season I won't be buying. Shame, used to love getting the new kit.* (Sparksy)

~~~~~~~

*Great new shirt, I will definitely be getting the home one, if not BOTH!! away shirt will come in handy for fancy dress nights out if I did wanna go as a bumblebee* (chris1821)

Without the prospect of any meaningful football for a couple of months, thoughts were turning back to the proposed bricks and mortar at the Copse Road End. However *Ciderspace* had to report that: 'Yeovil Town's plans to build a Food Store at the north end of Huish Park have now had an agreed delay in the planning process. The target date for the decision was due to be May 1st, but in the past month or so all has gone quiet on the application, with that date now having passed.
The club had been advised by SSDC that in order to comply with local and national planning policies, that they would need to provide information both on their future 'stadium' plans, as well as provision for replacement training pitches and community facilities......Without those being included in the application, or as separate but linked applications, it was likely that the Food Store application would be rejected. Thus it seems likely that the club have agreed to that delay in an attempt to avoid the application being thrown out. As yet there's no sign of the linked applications being submitted to SSDC.'

A bit of blow comes when Club Captain, Paul Huntington turns down his contract offer and returns to his Cumbrian roots by joining Preston North End. On his *Twitter* account he leaves a message:
*"I have now signed for Preston North End. Looking forward to a new challenge. Thank you for all the good luck messages. Thanks to all the Yeovil fans for the messages. It's been a pleasure to be captain and have enjoyed every minute! I really appreciate it."*
Ah well, life goes on.

In the last action of the season, Huddersfield Town grabbed the last promotion place by beating Sheffield United in a penalty shoot-out at Wembley. On their way they had beaten MK Dons in the semi- final. What a shame, such a nice Club.

Even before the ink was dry on the role call for League One next season, the bookies were writing us off. At *William Hill* we are quoted at 80/1 to win the division outright. Only Walsall have got greater odds at 100/1. The bookies think that Sheffield United at 6/1, MK Dons at 7/1 are most likely. New boys Swindon , 8/1 with Portsmouth , 9/1, Doncaster Rovers,10/1 and Coventry City 12/1. How many years on the bounce have we been favourites to drop out of League One? And how many times have we beaten the odds. Thanks *William Hill* you may just have ensured our safety again.

Like a mosquito in summer, (but not this Summer – still raining) what we needed was some new blood. It came in the shape of Sam Foley, 25 year old Irishman from Newport County. Gary Johnson said of his first signing:
*"Sam Foley is one that is probably a bit of a late developer in football. He can play in midfield and he can play up front, and he can play in the hole. He's a very good footballer, not only in scoring goals, but in creating goals. He's similar to like Gavin (Williams) plays really. He's young enough, he's keen, and he's looking forward to it very much. He just showed me that he wanted to prove himself at this level, and I think and he thinks that he is ready for that."*
Add to that a young 19 year old, Keanu Marsh-Brown, formerly with Oldham and Fulham and the news that Richard Hinds had agreed a new contract and things weren't looking too bad for so early on.

'Three's a happy trio, four's a crowd'. No I'd never heard that said either, but it seems appropriate as Nathan Jones felt a bit superfluous to requirements at Huish Park. He said:
*"I feel that my progression as a coach was stunted a bit and as I want to develop as a coach, the best place is away from Yeovil"*
Pastures new beckoned him to Charlton Athletic where he took up the position of Under-21 Professional Development Coach. Thanks Nathan for being the good old war horse in defence. We will never forget the 'step-overs'!

As one shuffled out through the door another trotted in. This time it was another former Oldham Athletic player, Rueben Reid. A Bristol born winger who should feel at home back in the West Country.

The power of the Twitter generation swelled the Yeovil Town coffers to the tune of £20,000. By registering tweets under the *'Fanpowerstadium'* banner Yeovil fans came out on top with the number of shouts they recorded (No I haven't got a clue what I am writing here, but hey £20,000 in anybody's language is fantastic). Chief Executive, Martyn Starnes spoke to the *Western Gazette* about the windfall:
*"For us to come through and win that prize is outstanding and I would like to offer my personal thanks to everyone that helped us get the money that will be very important to us. It was an extraordinary effort because it is not easy to get an extra £20,000 from anywhere. To have bought into that competition and to have won it is incredible."*

Director, Stephen Allinson who obviously did understand *Twitter*, said, via his account:
*"Brilliant - thanks to all the fantastic Yeovil Town fans. We are all proud of you. Thanks on behalf of the Directors."*
The Club shortly after listed three potential areas that the money could be spent on and invited supporters to vote for their personal choice. They were:

a)General refurbishment of Conference Centre first floor facilities.
b) Improvement to and additional supporter Stadium catering facilities.
c) Supporter infrastructure safety improvements.

What was it going to be then? No brainer really, it had to be b). More pies!

The promising loan player Joe Edwards returned to Bristol City and promptly penned a new contract at Ashton Gate. It must have been those bright city lights that lured him back.

The summer was moving rapidly on, no sun loungers were being used as it was still raining and the First Round of the League Cup had been announced. Home to Colchester United, Tuesday 14 August.
And before we knew it the full 2012-13 Fixture List was published. Coventry City at home for the first game. Who would have thought a few years ago that we would be taking in our stride the fact that we would

host the Sky Blues. For so long a Premiership club with a marvellous stadium, light years away from Huish Park, but now on the same field of play as us.

18 June: Swindon Town signed Andy Williams. Nothing more to be said from our side other than we'll survive. He wanted to have the last word however and in interview said:

*"A big reason why I came here was my ambition, because I have spent two seasons League One struggling at the wrong end of it and now I want to be in a team that is winning every week, and is creating chances for you. It was hard to leave Yeovil because I made a lot of friends there, and it is always hard to leave a club, but for me I want to move on and that was the ambition that I had. It is an ambitious club which is moving forward, and that is what I want to be part of."*

That's the joy of football, you can be down one moment and then high as a kite the next. Pain and pleasure they say are very much akin to each other. So, several waves of pleasure for us in the signing of former Bristol City defender, Jamie McAllister and former Doncaster Rovers and AFC Bournemouth striker, James Hayter, together with former Watford winger, Lewis Young, the younger brother of Man Utd and England winger Ashley Young.  There I am sure we all felt better for that.

Even more joy was to follow in early July. Byron Webster, signed by Gary Johnson at Northampton Town re-joined the Gaffer but to cap it all and not many Glover's fans thought that this could ever be possible, Marek Stech, by now a free-agent, hot foots it to Huish Park. This just shows the pulling power of the manager and also goes to the credit of Terry Skiverton who obviously sold the benefits of Yeovil Town to Marek when he was on his short month's loan in the previous season.
Fans were delighted and messaged:
*Has now signed yipee no more worrying about team being in bottom 4 this season.* (glover-tom)

~~~~~~

*Fabulous signing, so so pleased with this, the squad is really shaping up nicely, top half at the least I think, hooray no more simply avoiding relegation!* (nobrakes)

~~~~~~~

*Having had a little chat with Gary earlier this week i know he worked bloody hard to make this happen. In the end I think managed to convince*

*Marek that his career is best served playing week in week out with us than signing as a Championship No 2 right now.*

*Short term he may be able to increase his wages doing that but unless you play you won't make that leap to a Championship/Premiership No 1 with the rewards that come with such a move. Yeovil can help him make that jump. Well done Gary.* (Lector)

Not all was sweetness and light however. GJ was getting a bit 'grassed off' with the state of the training pitch at Alvington. Now that the top pitches behind the away end had been deemed 'not fit for purpose' the Club had concentrated their training sessions just down the road, much to the annoyance of Westland Sports who felt they had been muscled out of what had been their home ground. GJ said:

*"I am very disappointed with the state of our training ground at Alvington. We have not been able to get anywhere near it and will not be able to get anywhere near it for a while. To be honest it is a very poor piece of ground at this moment in time and the club should have an enquiry to see why that is.*

*"It has been unbelievable at Sherborne and we have been out there in all weathers with the ground prepared properly for us. It is important that we thank the school and their ground staff because without it we would have been in the manure."*

Worse was to follow when the pre-season friendly scheduled to be played at Huish Park on 21 July was switched to a neutral ground, Avenue Stadium, Dorchester because of 'adverse weather conditions'! Gary didn't seem necessarily to agree:

*"The season finished early and we cannot get a pre-season friendly on our pitch, of course I am disappointed. That was a good game against Plymouth and the club needs to have a look at it and see why that (Huish Park pitch) has not become available."*

Concerned *Green Room II* contributors had their say:

*What you've got to ask yourself is why a Conference South pitch appears to be able to cope with that (and in addition Hereford and Poole staged games against us without problems) yet we had to pull our friendly 12 days before it was due to be staged. That's not a little bit of "rain" - that has to be something far more structural - and when you add in the unavailability of the top pitches, and the Alvington pitch also not being ready, you've got to ask yourself what other clubs (at lower levels) are doing that we're not. Those are the questions I'd be wanting answers to if I was GJ.* (Badger)

~~~~~~~

*The drainage is poor in one part of the pitch. With a full time groundsman it's hard to see why there's a problem as no games were played on it during the recent monsoon.* (Oracle)

~~~~~~~

*Simply lack of professionalism once again. Oh to think of how well the club could be doing in the right hands.* (touched)

~~~~~~~

*The pitch could undo all the good work GJ has put into building a team unless they can adapt to it* (Wurzel)

A couple more loan signings in the form of Gozie Ugwu and Rohan Ince and that about saw us up to strength and before we knew it the Pre-Season friendlies began. (It was still raining)

*With all the rain we are having I'm wondering how good the drainage is at HP or are the team learning how to play water football* (glover-tom)

It seems that their designer flippers did the job because the team knocked up the following results:

Hereford 1 Yeovil 1,    Poole 0 Yeovil 2,    Yeovil 5 Plymouth 0,  Dorchester 0 Yeovil 3    Yeovil 1 Bristol Rovers 1,    Llanelli 3 Yeovil 5.

The poor old food store application got another kick in the teeth in early August. Not only criticised by just about every Parish, Town and District Council, together with the Tree Preservation Society and the Greater Crested Newts Foundation but now the Quedam Shopping Centre owners UBS Triton waded in with a body blow by announcing that they had big plans to expand the Quedam to include the now vacant Vincent's Garage site and build, yes you guessed it, a supermarket. Blimey how much food can we consume?

Yeovil's planning advisors, MWA had previously submitted as a ground for the Huish Park application that there were no suitable sites in Yeovil town centre. Woops!

Fans discussed the issue:

*Time for the club to accept the inevitable I think, the food store plans aren't going to happen. Now we need to cut our loses on it and focus on new revenue opportunities, otherwise a lot of time is going to be wasted.* (chris1821)

~~~~~~~

*Couldn't help but think though, wasn't the main reason for the apparent rejection of our plans on the basis that they didn't want another supermarket in the town? Surely they would increase revenue in the long term by helping our football club to expand?* (blachy71)

~~~~~~~

*I think we are desperate for a council to support the football club they do nothing at all but watch them get on the band wagon if the footballing side does well.* (rolfo)

~~~~~~~

*Keeping the land with the club and training facilities on site by working with the council to provide community facilities surely is the best option. Maybe in that circumstance the covenants can be partially relaxed to allow a catering outlet and maybe a sports outlet on the periphery of the site that pays rent and maybe one or two things integral to the stadium structure, along with the club's own supporters' bar.* (Cruncher)

~~~~~~~

*Could always convert HP into a massive Park & Ride* (jafa)


The pre-friendlies continued with  Newport 1 Yeovil 3 &  Yeovil 1 Stoke 1. Then on 6 August Yeovil Town went global. The media across the world clamoured for the latest story to come out of Huish Park. Had we signed Ronaldo and  Messi in a super swoop? It was quite simple really. We had no sponsor's logo to put on our new shirts.
*Ciderspace* reported the whole exciting affair under the banner headline:
*'Glovers Laid Bare As Johnson Gets Shirty Over Sponsor*
Yeovil Town manager Gary Johnson laid his club's problem out bare this morning, as part of the club's annual photo shoot. With the Glovers having yet to find a first team shirt sponsor for the 2012-13 season, the first team squad were asked to turn out for the team group with something missing - their shirts!

Johnson's logic was "no shirt sponsor - no shirt" as the players (but mercifully not the management staff) went topless for their team photo in the hope that the publicity gained would result in someone getting in touch with the club.

As reported last month, last season's sponsors Jones Building Contractors have declined the opportunity to extend their deal, and so the club have been wearing unsponsored shirts during all of their pre-season friendlies so far. Johnson told *BBC Somerset* that the club had received interest from prospective sponsors, but they were holding out for the right bidder. He joked that he'd insisted that he was one of the few to keep his own shirt on during the photo shoot:

*"It was my idea for the staff to keep their shirts on! Yes, it was (my idea). I think there's been a lot of interest from sponsors. But we feel that we're going to have a successful season. So obviously we need to make sure that the sponsors are paying the right sort of sponsorship money to be on our shirt. If we haven't got a sponsor at the moment then you can't wear the shirt."*

Johnson explained that he dropped the hint to the players that they would be asked to 'strip off' for Monday morning's session. However, claimed that his players reaction was to head down the gym to tone themselves up for the occasion:

*"I just felt that the boys have been working out over the last couple of days in preparation, and did a few press-ups before! It just highlights really that we are still looking for a sponsor. It's a little bit tongue-in-cheek of course; it's not serious. A few of the lads look okay and a few of them look like they need to get in the gym a bit more!"'*

He's just a bit canny that guy Johnson! That should bring the- would be sponsors a running.

One fan took the whole thing to another level:

*Re: No Sponsor? No Kit? No Problem!*
*Shame the ladies have been sponsored.* (stewies drinking pal)

Someone else who is going to need to share that canniness (is that a word?) is Chairman Fry. In an article in the *Sunday Independent* he spoke of his frustration at the lack of progress in his attempts to remove the restrictive covenants that he felt were hindering the Club's plans to develop the stadium and surrounding land.

*"It is very frustrating. We are up there with the best-run clubs in the country and have done things the proper way. But we need people to be helping us. There are restrictive covenants on Huish Park that need to be lifted to help us develop.*

*"How do we move forward with a restrictive covenant on the site? I seem to spend all my time going through hoops and hurdles. It has to be progression or die.*

*I don't want this to seem like a threat, but there are people who don't share our dreams. For instance, we haven't even got a training ground. There are no decent pitches in Yeovil.*
*We need to spend £500,000 on the pitch and I know it's a tough world out there. I have the dream to take the club higher. Fans don't want relegation battles every season, but to realise the dream we have to generate money. We have not gone to the council to ask for money, and I don't intend to, but we must get rid of that legal millstone around our necks."*

Probably the vast majority of Yeovil fans shared his concerns. Surely after 20 odd years it was time to remove those hurdles. It was quite understandable all those years ago that protection should be given to surrounding businesses, some of whom were in the fledgling stages themselves. The restriction on the sale of alcohol at Huish Park for example allowed the local public house to become fully established and self -supporting. Times had changed, the crutch was no longer required. Yeovil Town FC has changed and it should now be allowed to move forward in its off field activities to keep in step with the on field ones. Surely a specialist lawyer would be able to make out a case for these outdated covenants to be removed. We know that John Fry has been wrestling with this demon for many a year but perhaps now was the time to take some top quality advice. It would cost but think of the benefits.

You would think that with a potential 10 point deduction, a transfer embargo and still more than 58 million pounds in debt that Portsmouth would be taking it very carefully but no - why don't we take the whole squad to Portugal for
ten days for them to bond. What's another £100,000. Lucky for them they have encouraged one of their highly paid 'stars' to leave, saving £36,000 a week! Several others on similar money are not budging at the moment. What planet are Portsmouth on? We all know that professional football is not played on a level playing field but it certainly shows the chalk and cheese between us and Pompey.

For a moment we all took our eye off the ball as possibly the 'Greatest Show on Earth' came to town. London Olympics 2012 arrived with that magnificent sight of David Beckham speeding up The Thames with the Olympic Torch. (Sorry this was the only football connection I could think of and I put it in mainly to bring a smile to my wife who idolises him – can't see why!).

Some were looking forward to it more than others:
*Personally I am looking forward to anything with Jessica Ennis or Victoria Pendleton in. Or the Brazilian beach volleyball team!* (Dazz)

~~~~~~~

*The bit after the closing ceremony.* (therightstuff)

And the first Gold medal for G.B went to a Yeovil girl! A couple of fans posted:
*Well done Heather Stanning! Should we have a L1 Olympics table?* (simonfromlids)

~~~~~~~

*Peter Wilson got a gold yesterday at the double trap shooting. He is from Sherborne, but is a ytfc fan so that must count!* (puffpaddy)

9 August: GJ was having another go about the state of the pitch, suggesting to the *Western Gazette* that he was wanting a pitch with shorter grass on it, so his team had a better chance of playing their usual passing game, but that the club's groundsman was not carrying out his wishes:
*"One day someone will listen to me and make that grass short enough so we can get that opportunity (to play passing football)."*

It was not much to ask surely.

On 10 August the team could at last put their new shirts on. W&S Recycling of Poole  confirmed that they were to be the major shirt sponsors for the season. Tamburino, the Italian restaurant announced that they would be the name on the back.

Those that could tear themselves away from the T.V.  were 'entertained' with the last of the friendlies on 11 August :Yeovil 2 Exeter 2 : GJ was not terribly impressed with the performance and 'invited' the lads back on Sunday for extra training. A no nonsense Gary said:
*"They have to know what will happen when it doesn't quite happen on the pitch. We want to see a team in our image and we haven't seen it yet. We certainly didn't see it (against Exeter City).*
*"I just reminded them to make their minds up. If you want to be part of it, we need to see you in our image, otherwise your Huish Park careers might be very short. The lads now know how important Tuesday and Saturday is*

*to this club and if they want to be part of it they need to liven up."*

Gary had done the groundwork, all was now prepared for the start of what we all hoped would be the BIG one, the season to beat all seasons. He spoke to *BBC Somerset* the day before the first competitive match of the season, Colchester in the League Cup. Asked if the important thing was to get a strong start when the campaign commenced, he replied: *"We don't mind that at all. That's not a problem. We don't want to sneak up on the rails late on either. We want to get ourselves in a strong position nice and early, so that we give our supporters the benefit of seeing our performances early, and not just that, but to make sure that we feel confidence-wise that we're playing well enough to compete at this level."*

With Yeovil starting poorly in the two previous seasons and finding themselves at the foot of the table by Christmas, GJ added that he didn't want to continue with that pattern, even if the end result was relative safety on both occasions:
*"The goal is to compete and that is what you want to do. Being at the bottom of the table for most of the season is not competing. We need to compete at a level where it keeps everybody's interests and everybody feels that you've got a chance. With the play-off situation, as long as you're in the top half for most of the season, then you're going to be competing for at least a play-off place, and that keeps everybody's interest."*

Most thought we would do well to bob along in the mid table but opinions were mixed:
*So long as Gary stays this time, this promotion push is probably our most likely... the squad may not be too big but we have a lot of loan spaces should we need them (not that I want that. The squad is a league one/championship squad for sure with a lot of young players to grow which won't take long...*
*Very exciting to see how many goals we have scored in pre-season.*
(BucksGlover)

~~~~~~~

*Oi get off my patch. I'm Mr optimistic around here! Seriously though, this is a good squad, and we have had a free scoring pre -season and I honestly think we can do well, but to say as we are we can field a championship' ish squad is lunacy!* (Ytfc117)

~~~~~~~

*I think we lack quality in depth but IF we have few suspensions and IF we have few injuries we will finish in the top 10.* (Oracle)

~~~~~~~

*The better players are contracted now and can be supplemented with loans. Too often in recent years our better players have been the loans.* (therightstuff)

~~~~~~~

*Quite agree - I feel more confident now that we have a squad of contracted players.* (daveyboy)

While we waited for the 'starter's gun' (just threw an Olympic expression in there to show that I had been watching) one ale supping fan noticed that all was not well in the drinking tent:

*What's happened to the Green and White?*

*No - not the shirts or even the supporters group but the real ale that has been served in the tent. Last night it was just Tetley's and I have really tried to like it but no success. Green and White from a small local producer is just the sort of local mutual support that I think is needed. Not a lager or Guiness fan so it will have to be Cyder or the Arrow with real ale, faster service and lower prices. SAD!* (Rambler)

It's not a good idea to get between a guy and his pint:

*Like many others who used to be regulars in our "temporary" tent I got fed up with the mildew/dead fly infested pit and now spend my hard earned elsewhere.*

*The day Yeovil's answer to Egon Ronay reopens the VP bar to your average Joe Soap then I'm sure we`ll return en mass.  (Brizzol glover)*

## CHAPTER 7

# THE BIG PUSH

It was just as well that we fast forwarded for a few months. I hadn't realised how much had gone on since the return of GJ. Every day seemed to produce something new, some great results in that mini – season that we had and of course much coming and going in the close season. There was never a dull moment, that is if you forget the weather. Yes it is still raining.

The point I was going to make before I came over all meteorlogical was that I believe it was important to give as much of the build up and supporters response in order that we could see where we were coming from. They say that the darkest hour is just before dawn. A bit melodramatic maybe but I believe that many would see our darkest hour as being the Fleetwood replay leading up to the Christmas and New Year defeats. Then the dawn and who knows we may be just about to witness the rising Sun.

Put your sunglasses on and let us step into the bright, bright world that we hope will result in Yeovil Town's finest hour. (Blimey, I'm sounding like Winston Churchill now!)

Were we ready, were we really ready for the start the 2012-13 Season? Yes if the buzz around Yeovil was anything to go by. Everywhere people were asking eachother what they thought of Yeovil's chances. Most seemed pretty postive that they would be comfortable mid table. There was certainly a lot more optimism than for the start of the last couple of seasons. 'In Gary we trust' seemed to be the motto.

Tuesday 14 August 2012, 7.45pm Huish Park -1st Round League Cup. Opponents – Colchester United. Usually the first game is a league match but it's different this year. So we start with one of the bonus games. In the old non-league days we were often lucky to reach as far as Round 1 of any Cup so let's make the most of this.

And we did, 3 minutes 38 seconds in and Richard Hinds scores from a corner kick. He then added another just before half time. Yeovil breeze through, with Keanu Marsh-Brown adding a third on 79 minutes. It was just as well that we had our star International goal keeper on duty as he was called upon to make a couple of great saves in the second half. Only 1907supporters had the pleasure of watching but most certainly went home with a smile on their faces.

One *Green Room II* writer just about summed it up:

*Having seen most of the pre-season friendlies, it was great to see all the hard work and team spirit come out in last night's performance….. Pity about the low gate as the performance and style of football warranted larger support, perhaps preference of attending the upcoming Coventry game may have been the main factor. Looking forward to Saturday!!*
(RiffRaff)

There was one person who did not appear with a happy grin, in fact he didn't appear at all at the press conference following the game. Terry Skiverton came out to meet BBC Somerset and explained:

*"I think the manager has decided for me to come and do the press conference tonight. If he had come out, I think one or two hand grenades might have been thrown right into the mix of things. I don't think he wanted anything to detract away from the performance of the players tonight. But he's shot off straight from the ground, and even I had to take a step back. I don't think he's in a very good mood about something. But that will probably come out at a later date."*

When asked if it related to the state of the pitch, Skivo did not deny it. Fans debated it online:

*It's a bit embarrassing; I really do hope they sought something out as I fear we might lose GJ if we're not careful. Now the season has started is there much we can actually do about the pitch? (apart from cut the dam grass!)*
(puffpaddy)

~~~~~~~

*If it is the pitch & it certainly looked poor last night then I can understand GJ being upset. He has worked hard to improve the quality of the team & if it is all going to be undermined by someone who cannot do their job properly then he has every right to be unhappy.*

*Once again the board are looking at a cheap option, do away with family ties & get someone in with experience before it's too late.* (Lorraine)

A couple of days later when Gary had put the pins back in the hand grenades and had composed himself, he spoke to the press and spelt it out loud and clear:

*"You get all emotions, don't you, when you come into a football match. They all revolve around you trying to get the standards right. So you have high emotions of being happy, because the players got to a performance level where we've raised the standard. I'm looking for that from everywhere around the club, as are everyone else who is part of the club. Some people have different standards to others. I just want to keep pushing because I want this football club to go as far as it can. We've got to start acting and being like a League One club, which it has been for a little while now."*

*"So there are a lot of people who are trying to improve standards, and keep pushing and shoving, and I'm one that does that, and some of our Directors want to do that. But we have to get into those people who have not quite got those standards that we've got, and make sure that they raise them. If they do, then we'll all be happy."*

*"When you get a football team that is in your own image, and a team where you know how you want to play, then you've got to have the best facilities to do that. That includes training grounds as well. It includes maybe the Council trying to help us as well - do you know what I mean? At the moment we're having to travel half an hour up the road because our training grounds are impossible to train on."*

*"For a League One club, that is poor. There are people working hard to try to change that, but we need to try harder, and we need to get that right properly. That's because if you're going to play the type of football that I want us to play, then you have to train that way. Then obviously your surface is so important to the way your team plays."*

*"You can see we've got running power in our team, and you can see that we're trying to play one or two touch. The ball needs to get across the ground, and everybody knows how I want to play, and I think it reminded people that it needs type of surface. Sometimes I get a little bit disappointed when I see that it's not quite right for what we need, when we know the exact measurements. People sometimes have excuses of this, that and the other. But I don't want excuses, we need action. That's not having a go at any one person, or any one department. It's saying 'Look this is us, as a football club'. We need the best facilities that we can, out there and inside the stadium. We've got to keep pushing to improve our standard and that's the main thing."*

It seemed that it was going to have to be GJ's philosophy of exacting high stands of professionalism right across the Club or the old sloppy, amateur, non-league laid back style, of which, it seemed GJ was not prepared to be a part. A bit of pulling up by the boot laces was being called for. Would it be make or break?

Fans were in full support of Gary:

*Well! Having just listened to the interview myself, I think it's obvious that Gary is not a happy man. What was also obvious, IMO, was that he wasn't just talking about the length of the pitch. All I can say is, well said Sir, and I really hope it gets through to those who it was intended for.* (nobrakes)

~~~~~~~

*Gary's built a half decent side judging by the Colchester game.*
*The pitch is a joke, the grass is shorter in a cow field near my home!*
*For a manager to refuse to give an interview after his side has won 3-0 with an excellent performance worries me a lot.*
*I am very fearful he will walk. Wonder what odds I would get on Skivo being promoted back to manager?*(wurzel)

~~~~~~~

*The most interesting quote for me in regards taking the club forward was 'some of our Directors want to do that'......SOME!!!!! that's going to cause ripples....*
*How ironic it would be if the board's one good decision of recent times in bringing GJ in was what caused upstairs changes.* (touched)

Sandwiched amongst all this was the 2nd Round draw for the League Cup. For once we pulled out a nice little plum in the shape of West Bromwich Albion at home. Bring it on.

Meanwhile  Gary had  now turned his attention to the all important clash with Coventry City. He spoke  to BBC Somerset the day before the first league game:

*"It's a super game to have. For me, if I had to pick a team to play on the first game of the season, it would be somebody like Coventry at home. They're probably expecting to beat us. Hopefully the bookies have told them that we're hopeless as well. So we'll have to wait and see what sort of attitude they turn up with."*

Saturday 18th August 2012Well over 2,000 fans travelled from the Midlands, full of hope that their beloved Coventry would be able to chalk up a win and go on to bounce back at the first ask. We were equally all hoping for a great start, a win to put us on the road to a miracle promotion. With all these lofty aspirations filling the ground the atmosphere was electric. Wouldn't it be great if we could get 6,000+ supporters at Huish Park every time.

Ten minutes into the game and Coventry took the lead through Cody McDonald. From a free kick he was given too much space in the box and he calmly headed home. Fortunately, our contender for the Golden Boot award, Richard Hinds headed home the equaliser from a corner midway through the first half. Yeovil had the lion's share of possession as the 65% - 35% split showed but in the end it's scoring goals that wins games. 1-1, honours even.

Gary spoke to BBC Somerset afterwards:

*"I think we did enough to create enough opportunities to have won the game. They also created their opportunities. But the fact that we're saying that it could almost be two points lost against a club like Coventry is obviously meaning that us as a club are getting further forward."*

Some of the fans said:

*What a great day I have had, imo. I thought we played very well, tired towards the end but defo. deserved a draw against a side that should be in the top 6 come May, minor improvements to the refreshments meant I could get a pint of cider at half time(which is a big plus up)after Tuesdays win I am quietly optimistic for the season and just hope some of the missing fans will slowly come back so we can recreate the atmosphere of a few seasons ago. One thing I would say is that the players will run through brick walls for this club(on what I've seen so far) and they deserve the support of the fans. All of this is IMO!* (PETESANDALL)

~~~~~~

*Gotta say, haven't been this excited in ages about a YTFC squad. There's just so much youth and potential and PACE and stuff. I know promotion might seem a bit optimistic, but by the time we play Pompey I think we will know where we stand, and today was a good test of our promotion credentials.* (Ytfc117)

~~~~~~~

*I thought the terrace did a great job today in trying to create a good atmosphere with lots of pro-Yeovil songs including some old favourites that everybody could get involved in.*
*Almost felt like the atmosphere of old today. Well Done all.*(prideofsomerset)

One little footnote to the game was that little bit of extra flair from Coventry. To be exact a blue flare from one of their supporters that held up the game for a few moments in the second half. He'd be able to tell the Magistrates all about it later on.

218 expectant Yeovil fans headed up the A303 to West London on Tuesday 21August. Griffin Park, Brentford was their destination and Yeovil were to take on a team managed by Uwe Rösler who were being tipped for at least a play-off place. It was said that Uwe was doing wonders for the 'Bees' on a very small playing budget. Could be, we might think it quite large!
The possession statistics were almost identical to the Coventry game except this time in favour of Brentford. But it was Yeovil that got the goals.
James Hayter opened his account for the Glovers with a goal in each half and the Town were assisted with an own goal. Marek Stech chipped in with a fine penalty save and Yeovil ended a pulsating match 3-1 winners.

Have you ever heard it said that German's are bad losers? Well one fan on the forum thought Rösler was one:
*Just listened to his interview...... was all about how bad they were and how many chances they missed not a word about how well we played , What a wa....* (mojo)
Just say what you mean.

~~~~~~~

*Long may it continue. Like so many of GJ's past Yeovil teams last night was classic 'smash and grab' - listening to Bee's supporters going back they couldn't really fully understand what had happened.....'a game we should have won', 'we had so many chances', 'luck didn't go our way'.....and a few 'if we can't beat Yeovil....'*
*I say let them carry on underestimating us.....let the team do the talking. BTW having a first class keeper makes all the difference - he made sure we were in a position last night to take the win....top signing by GJ! (Green Commuter)*

Even though their manager may not have been impressed some of their fans were. 'Ilchlover' posted a couple of comments from the Bees forum:
*BTW, anyone who thinks that Yeovil are relegation fodder will be wrong. I didn't see Bury but Yeovil were a decent side and deserved their win, despite our short comings in helping them.*

~~~~~~~

*There's more: Gary Johnson (you know, the managerial option that we sneered at) has been working his magic at Yeovil again since his arrival last season. They are much improved and I fully expect them to have a decent season. They certainly aren't going down.*

~~~~~~~

*On leaving the ground last night it was really great when Brentford supporters were saying 'Well played' & a 'Very deserved win' 'Your team played some good football tonight, & All the best for the rest of the season.' It was just like leaving Notts Forest all over again on that wonderful night & made me feel proud to be a YTFC supporter.*
*Also the support inside the ground was brilliant, well done everyone.*
(Lorraine)

Speaking to BBC Somerset after the game, Gary Johnson was a little more generous than Uwe:

*It's a good win here because Brentford are looking to be one of the sides up there at the end of the season so to come and finish so clinically was superb - that's what you get from James Hayter."*
*"Early doors, people want to win games, and that first win is vital, to get it under your belt. It keeps our non-losing run going, which is nice for the confidence. The lads are getting more and more confident in each other. But that doesn't mean to say that you're not going to lose a game at some stage. That will be a test as well - how do we come back from a loss? But let's hope that it's a little while yet before we have to worry about that."*

Others were already speculating as to where the season may lead us:
*I was just wondering where everybody reckons we will finish come the end of the season. In my honest view depending on whether we can settle down and bang in some goals which is something that we always lack, I believe we will finish strongly. My heart says play off's but my head goes with between 9-12th. Obviously the play off's would be a massive goal for the club and it's all I want to see, so who knows hey?* (Tommyboy)

~~~~~~~

*Think we will finish 16th - 18th* (kota kinabalu)

~~~~~~~

*Mid table mediocrity with a stress free March and April would be fine by me.*
(Brizzol Glover)

~~~~~~~

*11th with 60 points.*
*Reid top scorer with 18 goals*
*job done!* (huishparkhughes)


~~~~~~~


*A top half finish has to be the aim this season. I'm going for 11th or 12th.*
*First aim as always is survival and 52 pts as is the case with most clubs in*
*our league. Play offs realistically may just be too big an ask for us this*
*season imo, but who knows what we could achieve if we get off to a good*
*start. Look what Stevenage achieved last season on a shoe string budget. It*
*can be done!* (Green and White Army)

It was obvious that we were not getting over ambitious even with 4 points
to our name. We were playing it cool.

25 August. We only went and did it again. Another away win, this time at
Scunthorpe United, 4-0!! We were top of the League. Don't panic !!! Goals
from Keanu Marsh-Brown, Reuben Reid and a pair from Gozie Ugwu
sealed all three points but as Ciderspace pointed out: 'This wasn't a one-
sided contest though by any stretch of the imagination. That was
demonstrated by a one-sided contest though by any stretch of the
imagination. That was the number of times that Marek Stech pulled off
stunning saves.'

At 3-0 the heavens opened and the damp Scunny faithful, having already
had their fill, left. A pity really because they missed a very confident Ugwu
round the keeper and slot in No.4. The important thing was that 113
Yeovil fans saw it and roared their approval.

Gary was a little nervous at the dizzy heights: He told BBC Somerset:
*It was fantastic for our supporters up there. They were singing "we are top*
*of the League" and I was thinking "oh my God, not this early, surely!" But*
*anyway, we're now there to be shot at. It's nice to be there and the lads*
*deserve their little bit of notoriety.*

And just to make sure we knew we were the best, a forum poster put:
*Also top scorers and best goal difference.*
*Got to feel good about being a glover at the moment.* (plannersimon)

Just to bring us back to earth it was reported that Joe Edwards, who had earlier been linked with a loan return to Huish Park, would not be returning. Shame really, he wasn't half bad.

Three games in and the first Managerial heads go on the chopping block. Poor old Andy Thorn of Coventry City gets the big 'heave ho' Not sure if it was because they couldn't beat the village pub side that is Yeovil Town and then John Sheridan of Chesterfield. Definitely not our fault this time.

A light diversion from our explosive start to the league arrived in the form of Premiership side West Bromwich Albion for the 2nd Round of the League Cup. The 'Baggies' ran out 4 – 2 winners after a magnificent display of good football from both sides. 6228 fans were treated to a good night out. For our part we saw something rather special in the form of Reuben Reid, an ex Albion player, who scored two goals to show them what they were missing.

Gary said afterwards:
*"If you're going to lose you'd prefer to lose to a Premier League side but I want them to think bigger and more positively when we come up against the better teams.We're going to come up against better sides in League One, so this was a little test."*

31August arrived and the transfer window closed without any activity on Yeovil's behalf other than advertising a vacancy. Wanted one skilled Groundsman. (who knows one end of a lawnmower from the other). Had Gary got his way?

I've got a bit of a problem at this point. I have just checked my research material and it seems that I have enough detail for about 2,000 pages more. If I felt that you were firstly, strong enough to carry around such a book and secondly, could actually wade through it before the 2015 -16 season started, I would have given it to you both barrels. However as my Publisher has told me that I am limited to less than two hundred pages because he's paying me £1 a word, (What? Do you think it's just footballers that earn outrageous money?) I have to draw in my horns and become more succinct. After all we have potentially 50 odd games still to go.

For those of you who may feel a little cheated, having come this far and had expected to enjoy every kick, spit and foul,  may I point you in the direction *Ciderspace.* Through dedication and sheer blood, sweat and tears the team that provide this internet site can take you back through their archives to March 1999. Everything you ever wanted to know about the Glovers since that time is contained on this site. I would like to say a big thank you to all involved for providing me with my daily fix.

What I propose to do is try and pick out the more important milestones of the season and where we have fallen a little short on performances or, heaven forfend lost, I shall be brief.

1 September and we were at home to Doncaster Rovers. I think it's right to say that over the last decade we have taken a fair few points off them. They probably see us as one of those boggy clubs, like we used to see Cheltenham. No surprise then that Yeovil continue the run and beat them 2-1. As always, it's a former player that come back to haunt and this time it was James Hayter with a header in the second half and then 'sub' Gozie Ugwu who literally 'chipped' in with a second. Billy Painter for Donny got the consolation prize.

GJ said in interview with BBC Somerset:

*"We scored our second goal after the substitution, which was nice, but Donny are never going to lay down and die - that's not their way. So they came back there right at the end, but obviously too little, too late. So I'm very, very pleased that it's another three points. Doncaster are going to be a very, very difficult team to beat because of their size. We had to be very brave in both penalty areas, and we were."*

On *Green Room II* fans were pleased with another good performance but there was a worry over the relatively small crowd of 3535.

*For those of you that follow Yeovil occasionally, this \*IS\* the season to come back and watch. GJ has put a talented, skilful and competitive squad together reminiscent of our Conference winning squad (Give or take one or two experienced players) and there will be plenty of Goals scored at home this season, more than for a few years now. You will get entertainment and value! UP THE GLOVERS! (Judd)*

4 September and a visit to the Mem to face Bristol Rovers in Round 1 of the Football League Trophy (The Johnstone Paint thing)
Always nice to stuff the Gas Heads. This time 3-0. Only downside was that Jamie McAllister was sent off for an off ball incident with former City colleague, David Clarkson, who apparently had driven Jamie to the ground that night. Perhaps a bit quiet on the way back.
A three match ban was handed down.

8 September. The first defeat of the season was administered by the 'Cherries' at Huish Park – Yeovil 0 – 1 Bournemouth AFC. Luke Ayling clocked up his 100th appearance for the Glovers. Harry Redknapp, fresh from the Crown Court, was with Bournemouth as a 'voluntary advisor'. Gary spoke of the team hitting a solid brick wall in their mental and physical fitness.
Forum fans were saying:
*I'm sorry but that was terrible to watch today. Never had the ball, very sloppy and hardly any effort on goal.*
*Might be back to reality if they play like that next week.*(Tommyboy)

~~~~~~~

*The point is, we have a very depleted and already tiny squad which is being pushed to the limit. Gary Johnson said after the Rovers game, we're mentally and physically tired. I don't care who you are, you're going to be knackered after playing 90 mins twice a week for 7 weeks at that level.*(FortressHuish_19)

As if this wasn't bad enough, news came that the Food Store application was to be delayed indefinitely.

The Hillsborough Disaster was on many fans minds following important findings. Forum fans wrote:
*After hearing the news today I'm pleased that football has come to learn that lies about Hillsborough have come out and as a Yeovil fan I would like to wish the families all the best in getting the result today and getting full justice they should have.* (glover-tom)
~~~~~~~
*This could have been any club and any fans and as such football fans as a whole should be happy with this result and should support the campaign for justice.* (Casuals)

<center>~~~~~~~</center>

*Glad the truth has finally come out but can't believe it's taken 23 years.* (macphisto)

The only bit of bright news that was to come for some time was a bit of a cash windfall from UEFA. To compensate clubs for the loss of international players during the Euro 2012 they were dishing out 100 million Euros. Our share - £4,241. Better than a poke in the eye with a sharp stick.

Sorry to say but Gary's 'brick wall' had been well built and for the next five games Yeovil couldn't manage a single point. Between 15 September and 2 October we lost consecutively to: MK Dons 1-0, Leyton Orient 4-1, Sheffield United 0-1, Preston North End 3-2 and Portsmouth 1-2. That's probably as much detail as you want and I wish to give. Horrible, horrible, horrible.

After defeat no.3 Byron Webster was big enough to say to BBC Somerset *"Personally, I'd like to apologise to the fans, because I was hopeless. We're all down. It was disappointing from start to finish and that's now three losses on the bounce. No disrespect to Leyton Orient, but we were confident coming here. We've let ourselves down and we've let the fans down that have come a long way. All I can say is to stick with us, and we will keep going."*

Also speaking to BBC Somerset was GJ:
*"People will be disappointed and quite rightly disappointed, because they want to see their team win. Maybe if most people were asked would you accept 11th place after seven games before the season started, then most people would have done."*
*"You don't want to lose three games. We've had two difficult away performances - I'm not making excuses for anybody, but I'm not going to cry over spilt milk after seven games. I know we've got the character here, certainly amongst the management staff, to turn it around."*

A few loan players were drafted into the squad to try and stop the rot. 21 year old Korey Smith from Norwich and a familiar name from the Big Club Up the Road, Joe Edwards together with Dan Burn from Fulham. Unfortunately they were not able to make an instant impact so as to turn the situation around.

A club record was set following the Preston game as Yeovil had never lost five games in a row since joining the Football League. What we, the fans, needed now was an Agony Aunt. Perhaps the Club understood our pain and promptly appointed a New Supporters Liaison Director. Stephen Allinson, a member of the Board since 2001 who would now be acting as the club's main contact for the Football Club's Customer Charter. Speaking via the *Green Room II* forum, Stephen said of his plans:
*"I do intend to set up (quarterly) meetings with our various groups and we will see how they develop. Obviously some aspects of any business are things which must be kept in the Boardroom but I also hope I can be a conduit for fans. I am happy for anyone to ask to see me at a game."*

Most fans wished him good luck and hoped that this would be opportunity to open up a more two way dialogue between supporters and the Club:

*Some friends and I met him on a tube after a game last season (might have been Wycombe). He seemed a decent, sensible bloke who was willing to have a discussion about the club with people he'd never met. Deserves a chance.* (Rich_the_Glover*)*

~~~~~~~

One or two thought he may have been handed a poisoned challis:
*I like S.A. or 'Big' Steve as he's known in certain circles. He's a braver man than I though.*
*Not for all the tea in China etc... .* (Salad)

Unfortunately after a bright start it seemed to fizzle out and he stopped posting on the *Green Room II.* That was a shame really as a chance had been missed to reach out to some fans who felt they were being ignored by the Club.

Of course it could be worse. We could be Colchester United. Sitting 22nd in the league, worst start to a season for 75 years, without a win to their name. What could they do? Of course, sack the manager, John Ward

I promised I wouldn't put anyone through the heartache of the grizzly details of the last six matches and I won't except to say that Lewis Young was stretchered off with what looked to be a nasty injury and Byron

Webster picked up his fifth yellow card and would be suspended for the next game.

Fortunately Lewis Young had not broken any bones but the ankle ligament damage might keep him out for a few weeks. Also fortunately we still had a place in the squad for another loanee should we need it.

Now was a time to hold the collective nerve. Some could, some couldn't. The Forum was like a big jelly, wobbling all over the place:
*Six in a row.*
*It's all gone horribly wrong and the club is in free-fall at the moment. It is not that the players do not have the ability, considering our budget Gary has put together a decent, competitive side. We are now heading back to our usual pre- Christmas position though very rapidly. The team is just not performing as it should and getting the results.*
*At the end of the day, results are all that matter.*
*Sort it out Gary.* (Wurzel)

~~~~~~~

*May I question how we could get into this mess after such a great start! We started off with some great form! Including pre- season we didn't lose a game in a good 10 matches or so! We looked professional also! Now we just look too relaxed and heads dropping! It just frustrates me how we can do so poor recently! You don't lose ability, so how could the players of done so great and then just dropped! They all have the ability but something isn't right! Needs to be sorted out quickly!* (glover in a glove 69)

And another one bites the dust or in this case two. Bournemouth lying in 20th place, having given the kiss of death in a vote of confidence earlier, axed Paul Groves and Shaun Brookes from the management. The big money was on 'Our Arry' to take over.

Two days before the arrival of  rudderless Colchester GJ added yet another loan player to the squad. This time a 22 year old striker from Carlisle, Paddy Madden. *Ciderspace* reported that he was mostly used as an impact substitute at Brunton Park but with only 2 goals in 36 appearances perhaps not much of an impact. Little interest was generated on the forum and the lad hardly  registered a post:

*Paddy Mallen has arrived on loan:* (Badger)

~~~~~~~

*So have we signed, Paddy Madden or Badgers Mallen* (jafa)

~~~~~~~

*Is this a sign of the times that we are now getting loans from Carlisle?*
*(puffpaddy)*

~~~~~~~

*Little bit desperate?* (NBGlover)

Gary said:
*"We'd earmarked him as like an Adam Stansfield type. The minute we*
*started feeling that we needed that type in our squad, and he became*
*available, the two came together and we thought we'd better get this done.*
*He was very very keen to come down and show what he can do. So I picked*
*him up myself at Bristol Airport on (Thursday) morning and brought him in.*
*So I'm looking forward to it. He's had a good training session. So he looks fit,*
*he looks lively, and he'll certainly be involved on Saturday in the squad."*
Like Adam Stansfield – say no more.

Still the worries persisted but a voice of reason came from the Forum:

*Ladies and Gents - the time has come for us to all ABU - to unite and stand*
*fast and strong against the on rushing tide of pessimism and angst that our*
*recent run of form has caused.*
*No losing streak lasts forever.... We can and will get a result on Saturday,*
*this rot will be addressed. 3 points and the world seems a better place.*
*So here's to us showing Gary and the boys that we are all YTFC and that we*
*will stand by them through this. They need to know that as long as they pull*
*on the green and white and give us 100% that we'll be there alongside them*
*giving them 100% in return.*
*We need to show Gary he's home - that the grass is greener here.*
*So to whoever maybe reading this from the club – let's leave the loans on the*
*bench, get the team that did so well at the start of the season back, same*
*players same formation, let's get the ball down and pass and move, and the*
*result will come.*(Old Green Eyes)

In some however, the paranoia was taking hold:

*So, all of you "In GJ we trust" followers, who is to blame for the current predicament?*
*The Board? The players? The fans for not turning up? But wait, there is one missing from that list........*
*I was concerned earlier in the season when Johnson, a few games in, moaned about the pitch and then moaned about the lack of support from fans. Perhaps he could see the limitations of the squad and started to prepare his "reasons" for leaving the club. Maybe I am being pessimistic, but he has walked before.* (GloverHiBee)

There were others who thought he might be on his way again, after all, the Bournemouth job was vacant. This was definitely time to believe that GJ was a Somerset boy at heart and that Yeovil was his first love.

Thank goodness Saturday arrived. Thank goodness it was Colchester who also arrived. The tide turned at last and it was the quiet loanee, Paddy Madden, that made the difference, weighing in with a couple of fine goals to instantly equal his Carlisle record. James Hayter, who had a result of his own over the weekend, becoming a father of a baby daughter, celebrated with the third goal in the 3-1 victory. Only 3002 watched the game, including 118 Colchester fans. After such a poor run it was no surprise that the crowd was as sparse as it was, but still very disappointing for League 1. In fact it was our lowest attendance in the Football League. Back up to 13th place, unlucky for some but I guess we would take it.

A relieved GJ in interview with BBC Somerset said:
*"It is a little bit of a monkey on your back when you've lost a few games on the trot....... I was really, really pleased with firstly our preparation throughout the week, and secondly - thank God - we've stopped this run of defeats."* *"That (third goal) was testament to his* (James Hayter)*game really, and a reward for his game. He worked so hard, and I wish he could have a baby every week! Then he and us would be fine!"*

Asked about the rumours that he might be jumping ship, he put more than a few minds at rest when he replied:
*"I'm loving it here. I'm loving my partnership with Darren (Way) and Terry (Skiverton) and we're all working hard. It's a club that I wanted to come back to and it's a club that we want to try to get back up that table. There's nothing in it whatsoever. Nobody has spoken to me. I've not spoken to*

*anyone else. So there's absolutely, at this moment in time, nothing in it. So I'd be stupid to be thinking about anything else other than Yeovil, and making sure that Yeovil are competitive."*

Within a couple of days it was announced that Eddie Howe would take charge of Bournemouth, so big sighs of relief.

It is amazing what a win can do for confidence in a team and no less so with the fans. The Forum was much steadier:
*Yes, a better display today, but every time the opposition attack I hold my breath.*
*Paddy looked good, and could of had three.*
*Long way to go yet, so keep the faith.* (saxon)

~~~~~~~

*It was good to see us back to attacking football yesterday along with two up front. Madden had a good debut and seemed to team up well with Hayter if this partnership continues to work then be good to see us sign him on a longer loan but as with all loans you cannot tell after just one match so hopefully if it works let's hope we can get him longer. (isistoleague)*

Next up was due to be Torquay at Plain Moor in the Johnstone Paint Trophy but the lads and the fans had a night off due to the waterlogged pitch. (Still raining!)
With the fixture postponed we were able to go into the draw and  pulled out Wycombe Wanderers at home. If all went well we could see our way to a final. *Green RoomII* followers were a little split:
*We are now one of only three League 1 sides left in the southern half of the draw. The others are Brentford and Leyton Orient.*
*Wembley should be the aim.* (will_ran)
~~~~~~~
*Forget about the JPT...concentrate on pushing for the best league finish possible* (Wurzel)
~~~~~~~
*I appreciate where you're coming from, but I remember people saying "Ignore the FA Trophy, we should rest players and focus on getting into the league". The JPT could be just the thing to give us a similar kick start, and a Wembley trip and a day out for a final could well get people interested in attending again.*(RoboChap)

The trip to Prenton Park on 13 October was eagerly anticipated. Tranmere Rovers had got their season off to a flyer and were riding high at the top of the league. If we could just topple them it would give us a hell of a boost.

However and I hate to use an old football cliché, but it seems appropriate, this was a game of 'two halves'. It would be possible to throw in an old film title as well. The Good, The Bad and the Ugly!.

It only took Paddy Madden 9 minutes to get on the scoresheet and with fellow Irishman, Sam Foley adding to it on 29, things were going well. Then it got a bit feisty with Tranmere's captain, Wallace appearing to elbow Korey Smith in the face. Either it was or it wasn't but a yellow card was wrong whichever way. You could bet your bottom dollar that Wallace's let off would come back and bite us. Sure enough on 45 minutes he headed in from a free kick. Life became difficult in the second half and on 51 minutes they had levelled. Worse was to come when Joe Edwards picked up a second yellow card and the backs were to the wall. Almost inevitably Tranmere powered on and scored the winner on 79 minutes when Yeovil fell asleep at a free kick.

Skivo did the honours after the game and said:
*"I thought for the first 40 minutes we were outstanding today. I thought that we could have had maybe one or two more goals in that period. But you can see why Tranmere are top of the League. The timing of their goal right on half time seemed to knock the stuffing out of us a little bit. The positives are that our start was excellent. But it was just that 15 or 20 minute spell in the second half, where we didn't stand up to a good Tranmere team, where their fans really got behind them*

One supporter who was looking at the Glovers with fresh eyes wrote on *Green RoomII:*
*My first game of the season today and I seem to have caught both the very good and very bad of our side this season. Going forward we looked a threat and were clinical with our chances. Couple of chances in first half where Madden perhaps should of squared it but went for it all himself only to miss. But who can blame him with the form he is in?!*
*Defensively we were shocking at times. It's almost like we could do the hard stuff like last ditch tackles timed to perfection and blocks and then fell asleep at a corner to gift them a third goal albeit a goal with the aid of a potential handball. But, it wouldn't of been a contentious point of reference*

*had we not been so 'school boy' in our concentration to let Holmes just walk into acres of space in our box.*
*Overall we were our own worst enemy. Tranmere were a neat and tidy side and simply due to their start should get playoffs but I can't see them winning the league. When they eventually lose I fancy they'll hit a bad patch of form and slip down a little. (Cheshire Glover)*

As the games mounted up, so did the injuries. Luke Ayling had missed the Tranmere game with a hip problem and now another squad member, Nathan Ralph would have to have surgery to remove a cyst on his knee. Added to that was a continuing problem for Gavin Williams and a calf muscle issue. Gozie Ugwu had earlier pulled a hamstring and Lewis Young would be out long term with his ankle/knee injury.

Despite the injury list we had enough players able and willing to take a penalty in an exciting shoot-out finish in the re-arranged Johnstone's Paint Trophy against Torquay, after the match had finished 2-2. We marched on into the Quarter Final of the Southern Section. With only being four games away from a Wembley final, surely this could be our best ticket to the stadium, bearing in mind our hot and cold league form.

Moving swiftly on to Saturday 20 October and we were due to 'entertain' Bury. Strange expression that, we were hoping to do more than 'entertain' them!
Before the game *Green RoomII* fans predicted the result:

*4-1 Yeovil Hayter x2, Maddden and Upson*
*Att: 3492 (sam.watts). Optimist!*
~~~~~~~
*1-3 just like we always do against teams who can't win a one ticket raffle!*
*(swat). Pessimist!*
~~~~~~~
*Saw a sign outside the betting shop in town centre this morning Yeovil 2 Bury 1- bet £10 win £90, so will say 2-1 to Yeovil and no I did not put a bet on. (dbail). Well done, you win the prize but unfortunately not the 90 quid!*

Yes, Yeovil as predicted dispatched Bury 2-1. Byron Webster and Sam Foley, knocking them in. It was also nice to see Adam Lockwood, from our

Conference winning team at Huish Park again. Fortunately he didn't alter the result.

Just like buses, one win and another two came along. By the end of the following week Yeovil had travelled to Shrewsbury Town and then Crewe Alexandra and won 3-1(Paddy Madden 2 & James Hayter) and 1-0 (Byron Webster). That was more like it.

The sun was shining again, well metaphorically. In reality I think it was still dampish.

Optimism flooded onto the *Green Room II:*

*I know it's still early days but it's nice to still be in the reckoning at the end of October instead of people already telling us we're definitely going down. 4 wins in 5 in the league and a first clean sheet since god knows when. All the praise in the world to the players and management for the way we've turned it around.* (FortressHuish_19)

~~~~~~~

*As Sir Gary said - "sometimes you have to play like Barcelona and sometimes you have to play like Ragarse Utd, you don't mean to but it sometimes happens" Well done to all the team ( staff and players). Feeling more comfortable now but let's continue to press on lads.*(daveyboy)

Oh and we got Preston North End away in the draw for the 1st Round of the F.A.Cup. What a surprise, away again!.  In years gone by this tie would have generated a great deal of excitement. Giant Killers, Yeovil Town pitched against the mighty P.N.E. What a clash! Now, it's lost some of its gloss. Not too many could get over excited about it.

Remember that lad from Coventry with the artistic flare? Well, the Magistrates remembered him as well. It cost him £300 and a three year banning order. Imagine three years without being able to watch Coventry City. Bliss!!

Another loan player was drafted in and believe it or not Gary Johnson senior has signed up Johnson junior. Not his junior but a Daniel Johnson from Aston Villa. He would be with Yeovil for a month.

A bit of a worry on the horizon was that Paddy Madden was due to return to the frozen north after playing away at Crewe. Technically the loan ran until after the Preston cup tie but it was thought unlikely that Carlisle would allow him to play that one.

Manager Gregg Abbott was saying to the *Carlisle News and Star* the week before the loan ended:
*"Paddy is going to come back with goals and confidence under his belt. He is going to be looking to force his way into the team. It has been a bit stop-start for him here with his injuries and stuff, but it's fantastic news that he is scoring goals, and that is another boost we can look forward to – an unexpected one. He (Gary Johnson) will obviously want to keep him but at the minute it's looking like he is going to be coming back. If he can reproduce his form for us then that's all the better."*
When asked by BBC Somerset about the situation, Terry Skiverton said:

*"That's to do with the gaffer. He had the foresight to bring him in. Paddy has done a fantastic job for us so far, as well as James Hayter. I think those two have been linking really well. I think our delivery has been excellent for Paddy Madden. So he fits into our team quite well at the moment. But there's no news from me - it's just something that will be on going with the clubs at the moment. It's something that for the gaffer is a priority that he'll be looking into, to try to extend Paddy's loan."*

Then on the day we played Crewe and prepared to say goodbye to our goal scoring machine, Gregg Abbott said

*"We're going to get the weekend out of the way, and then we'll go with that one. What we did with Paddy was we sent him out to get some football, to see where he was, and to see if he could find some consistency and some goals and he's done that. So he's caused us a problem that nobody could have foreseen before he left. But that was the idea of the loan period, and so it's a win-win all round. But I'm going to speak to Paddy and probably Yeovil on Monday, and see where that one goes."*

Then on the Monday Gregg Abbott said it would be sorted out within the next 24-48 hours. Give us a break! We, the fans were biting our nails to the quick and generally getting in quite a state. Postings flooded the *Green Room II*:
*The fans on their forum want him back, let's hope their management don't.* (tom_h_n )

~~~~~~~

*The other thing is, if he keeps scoring we could potentially take a play- off spot that Carlisle could have. Really can't see them letting us keep him longer.* (puffpaddy)

# THE
# ADAM STANSFIELD
## FOUNDATION

Adam at Villa Park – always with a smile on his face.

**About The Foundation:** Following Adam's death on 10th August 2010 Adam's wife, Marie and his immediate family were completely stunned and overwhelmed by the amount of support which was displayed by football fans, not just from the clubs he played for but from all over the country. The family became very aware that people wanted to do charitable/fundraising activities in Adam's memory. They decided that Adam's death should not be in vain and in September 2010 the Adam Stansfield Foundation was formed.

**Foundation Aim:** The promotion of community participation in healthy recreation for the benefit of children and young people up to the age of 16 residing in Devon, Herefordshire and Somerset by the provision of grants and facilities for playing football.

**Make a Donation:** Please make cheques payable to 'The Adam Stansfield Foundation' and post to The Adam Stansfield Foundation, PO Box 174, Tiverton, Devon EX16 0ET.

We at the foundation wish to promote awareness of Bowel Cancer and help in the quest to save lives of people in the UK and beyond. Think about your own health or family members and consider the impact Bowel Cancer could have.

THANK YOU.

*LEADING BY
EXAMPLE:
Captain, Jamie
McAllister at home
to Coventry City*

*ONE FOR THE LADIES:
Anyone want to sponsor us?*

*STECH AT A STRETCH:*
*Marek saves away at*
*Brentford*

*ANOTHER FOR HIS COLLECTION:*
*James Hayter scores against*
*Leyton Orient*

*IN CONTROL:*
*Luke Ayling at home*
*to Brentford*

*FEEL THE BURN!*
*Byron Webster celebrates*
*his goal against Crawley Town*
*with help from Dan Burn*

*I MOUSTACHE YOU A QUESTION....*
*What is that on your top lip?*
*Gary sports a 'tache' for Movember*

*LUCK OF THE IRISH:*
*Away fans at the last game of*
*the season at Bury*

*WHAT DO YOU MEAN YOU CAN'T SEE?*
*Byron Webster and Dan Burn causing*
*problems at home to Crawley Town*

*ON THE ATTACK:*
*Kevin Dawson starts a run*
*at home to Crawley Town*

*I DON'T BELIEVE IT!*
*Sam Foley goes close*
*against Brentford*
*at home*

*WHAT A BEAUTY!*
*Ed Upson scores a*
*smasher from a free*
*kick against*
*Brentford at home*

*A TRUE STRIKER:*
*Paddy Madden scores*
*against Leyton Orient at*
*home*

*GIVING THE SLIP:*
*Paddy Madden does it again*
*against Sheffield United away*

*PERFECTION:*
*Kevin Dawson scores the opening goal*
*against Sheffield United in the 2nd leg of*
*the semi play-off at Huish Park*

*HAPPINESS:*
*Kevin Dawson*
*style, after his goal*

*WE'VE ONLY GONE AND DONE IT!*
*Gary, Skivo and Dazza celebrate*
*reaching the final of the play-offs!*

*KEEP OFF THE GRASS!*
*Not this time as fans*
*celebrate getting to*
*Wembley*

*LET THE FUN BEGIN:*
*Wembley here we come!*

*KARL ROBINSON – WHO?*
*Marek Stech shows the banner*
*to the Sky T.V. pundit*

*WEMBLEY WAY:*
*The fans begin to arrive*
*at the famous stadium*
*– 19th May 2013.*

*TAKING ONE*
*FOR THE TEAM:*
*Captain, Jamie McAllister*
*takes a bash on the nose.*

*OUTSIDE RIGHT:
Paddy puts the
Glovers in front
against Brentford
at Wembley*

*LOOKS JUST AS
GOOD FROM
THIS SIDE:
Paddy Madden
scoring Yeovil's
first goal*

*CHEERS!
Yeovil fans
celebrate Paddy
Madden's goal*

*A BURN-ING DESIRE:*
*Dan Burn scores*
*Yeovil's second goal*

*RISING HIGH:*
*Dan Burn's goal again*

*WE ARE GOING UP!*
*Jamie McAllister lifts the*
*Play-Off Winner's Cup*

*CHAMPIONSHIP BOYS:*
*Paddy Madden, Dan Burn*
*and Marek Stech*

*WINNERS – YES WE ARE:*
*Joe Edwards and*
*Matthew Dolan*
*confirm it*

*MAGIC JOHNSON:*
*Manager Gary Johnson*
*lifts the trophy*

*IT'S COMING HOME:*
*The open top bus brings*
*the heroes home*

*Can't we just kidnap him , and keep him in hiding?* (PETESANDALL)
*Seems like it's all about the money, ie. that they don't want him back but can't be too blatant about that because it takes away their bargaining power. I would guess he was relatively cheap for the month he was here because he was unproven, and that we have made a fairly decent improved offer ref. wage contribution to continue his stay at YTFC, but Carlisle are probably waiting a bit longer in case another club feels his stint with us makes him worth a punt on a better offer than we can manage.* (Cruncher)

By 31 October Gregg Abbott had got himself in quite a stew it seems. The Carlisle fans were baying for Paddy to return but the management couldn't make up their minds: Talking to the BBC Abbott said:

*"I don't think there's any right decision with Paddy (Madden). If he goes there and scores goals, then we'll probably live to regret that. If he stays with us and doesn't get into the team then he doesn't play, then we'll probably live to regret that. So it's one of those - I wish we had a crystal ball. But what we're going to do is to try to make the right decision as we sit here now. It's a difficult one and it's not straight-forward. I'm sure there will be arguments for and against the situation that goes on with Paddy."*

*"Some of it has to be considered for Paddy's benefit and we also have to think about what's best for the club. Obviously Yeovil are involved in at all as well, so it's not as cut and dried as you would think. I've given my opinion to John (Nixon )*(Managing Director) *and he is talking about what happens next to Yeovil. We'll see where we are at in terms of what they want to do with him and what the state of play is and then we'll decide what we think is the right thing to do."*

This was doing just about every Yeovil fans head in. We were tearing our hair out (those that had any left after supporting Yeovil for years). Paddy, however was thinking of getting his styled. In a *Twitter* post he asked his followers to recommend a hairdressers in the town of Yeovil.  Did this mean????
Yes it did!! 1 November and *Ciderspace* broke the news that Paddy Madden's loan would be extended until the New Year. Well done GJ. BBC Somerset asked him if he would be looking to make the move permanent in the New Year. Gary played a little coy over that one. He was equally

reticent to say whether Carlisle would give permission for him to play in the Cup.

Fans rejoiced, danced in the streets, drove around the streets sounding horns. Well that's probably what they would have done in Italy. Too bloody cold and wet here but in our hearts we were doing the same. Indoors in the warm Forum posters were sharing the news:
*Carlisle have lost the plot. Why would you loan a player to a team who is going to be competing with you for a play- off spot? (provided we keep the Madden form up).* (puffpaddy)

~~~~~~~

*Perhaps but I have heard Paddy doesn't want to go back - would you want to force a player to stay when he doesn't want to stay?* (DazTaylor)

~~~~~~~

*Carlisle fans slightly pissed off with this decision.* (NBGlover)

~~~~~~~

*The funny thing is that upon his arrival, the Carlisle fans on Twitter were telling us that we'd signed the worst striker ever, who was only good enough for the Conference. So they seem to have changed their tunes, without seeing him play in a single match since!* (Badger)

~~~~~~~

*Another great piece of work by our board and GJ.* (garyspeed)

All that excitement couldn't last and it didn't! Yeovil Town fell at the first hurdle in the F.A.Cup. 3-0 to Preston North End at Deepdale. While many would have been deeply disappointed at both the score and the performance, many more were probably thinking that hey! we were never going to win the F.A.Cup, let's keep our eye on a more manageable prize – the League Trophy. That's garbage really, a run in the F.A.Cup is one of the greatest things to most clubs but we have to say something to lessen the pain. And just to add to our burden, Ed Upson was red carded and had to serve a four match suspension. Bugger!

Cup-tied, Daniel Johnson, Korey Smith and Joe Edwards were all in the line- up to face Stevenage at Huish Park. Upson of course was missing but so to was Byron Webster, out with a hip flexor muscle problem. Like Tranmere Rovers, Stevenage had got off to a flying start to the season and would move into second place if they could beat the Glovers. They did, 3-1. *Match Magazine*, Player of the Month for October, Paddy Madden scored the Glovers goal. Only 2900 braved the freezing Tuesday night weather to attend.

Gary bemoaned the inconsistencies of his young squad. Talking to BBC Somerset after the game he said:

*"We will never have a better chance to beat a Stevenage team who are up in the top three or four as I thought we outplayed them in the first half. But that's this division and the inconsistencies of it, and that's our team with the inconsistency of it. We were in 10th spot, and we could have been looking at 9th or 8th, and then going into Saturday's game looking at a play-off place. But life or football is not like that, and it certainly didn't happen today."*

It seemed that many Yeovil fans were taking this winning a couple and losing a couple in their stride:

*Last year we were languishing in the bottom half and too be honest come christmas we were all wondering where points would come. It is a tough league and we have done well to stay in this league when you look at other clubs and where they are now. Remember Rushden?*

*11th place is pretty good all things considering. We are going to lose matches but we are capable of winning matches as well. As said the problem is we have such a small budget and small squad. Mind you when we go on about crowds Preston aren't pulling that many in now they are in our division and when you think a few years back Oldham were getting around 10.000 at home and now lucky to get 4,000 so it is not just us that have seen gates fall.*

*Anyway let's put Stevenage and Preston behind us now and look forward to Saturday when hopefully we will get back to winning ways.* (isistoleague).

Another was not so laid back about the lack of support the club was getting:

*This might seem a bit strong and possibly controversial, but with the crowds continuing to dwindle we don't deserve to be a football league club with crowds like we got last night. GJ can only do so much. The Town have taken the clubs football league status for granted. What do people want? GJ has got us playing some good football and we are scoring goals. Yes, we lack consistency, but when you are working with a small squad and a limited budget what do you expect.*

*If we were to reach the Johnstone Paint Trophy Final at Wembley you watch all these so called Yeovil fans come crawling out of the woodwork just like they did when we reached the play off final. Rant over!*

*Let's hope we bounce back in style on Saturday with 3 pts and a 90 minute performance. Keep the faith and get behind the team as that is all that matters! (Brizzol Glover)*

An extra 195 punters poured through the turnstiles on the following Saturday 10 November to see one of the least glamorous of our rivals, Hartlepool. Joe Edwards scored the goal in a 1-0 win which had to be ground out. Still what do they say. It's the best teams that can win when they are not playing well. 25 points on the board, half way to the usual 50 safety line, six games to the half way stage and 11th in the league. Most would settle for that.
Most, did not include GJ:

*"I'm the one who has been doing all screaming to the players over the last few days about where we should be. I genuinely believe that we've got a group of people who can be competing for a play-off place. I'm not going to change that view until mathematically we can't do it. I'm going to keep pushing and shoving, cajoling and supporting the players we've got."*

Debt ridden Portsmouth lost their hard pressed manager, Michael Appleton when he jumped ship and headed for Blackpool. Former Yeovil striker, Guy Whittingham was appointed Caretaker Manager. Sorry Guy!

Don't you just hate Swindon. Always the big I am's. Always over spending, pushing the rules beyond their limits and always on the local T.V. Manager Paolo Di Canio must have his own hot line to the media. Oh and doing far too well, scoring far too many goals and due to play us at the County Ground on following Saturday. Just knew somehow it would end in tears, short term for us and maybe long term for them.

As a little aside, it was a proud moment on 14 November when Steven Caulker won his first full England international cap playing against Sweden to celebrate the opening of their new national stadium, the Friends Arena. Was this the first time Yeovil had a player go on to represent the England senior team?

Saturday came and went. Yeovil Town came to Swindon and went empty handed. 4-1 to 'Swindle'. James Hayter scored for the Glovers and an Andy Williams guy scored for the others. We won't go into that. Credit must go however to the 453 Yeovil supporters who gave it their all throughout the game. With a bit more vocal support like that at Huish Park it could be formidable.

Crowd size was exercising the minds of not only the fans. They had for some long time been putting forward theories as to why the supporters were not coming back. Some thought it was an overall lack of 'match day experience', with poor refreshment outlets, no social club and a lack of communication with the Board. Others put it down to the 'recession', alternative entertainment available or just the weather. One or two had a feeling it was something to do with the football.

It seems that the Club had noticed the empty seats and the gaps in the Thatcher's Stand. Chief Executive Martyn Starnes speaking to the Club's website said:
*"We are obviously concerned at the numbers attending Huish Park recently and we need to rebuild our home support. It's a challenging environment for most clubs at the moment and we recognise it's going to be a tough task to return our average attendance to 5,000 but we have to set ourselves a target that will enable us to move forward with our ambitions."*

To set the 'Target 5000' in motion the Club issued vouchers to local schoolchildren who were invited to take Mum or Dad along to the next game with them for £10.
Future plans will include Family Packages, Ticket Bundles, and promotions driven by club sponsors. The club already has in place two slots for their established Kids For A Quid promotions for later in the season. In addition, the forthcoming midweek Football League Trophy tie against Wycombe Wanderers has reduced tariffs throughout the stadium.
GJ was obviously going to feel the impact of lower attendances in his budget for the January transfer window and said:
*"Something has got to give if the figures don't match up and it could be anything. If you are looking at it from a business point of view, I have been given a budget based on gates of 4,000 and if we don't get that then it is going to be difficult."*
Little old Gary became a tad nostalgic when he said:

*"I often go back, and funnily enough I've shown the lads some of our games in the past, so that they know what me, Terry and Darren have got in our minds and what we are looking for. It shows the big crowds at the games here. They were very noisy and they were very supportive, and they were very up for it. And it does create a great atmosphere. It would be lovely to get back to that point. But you have to win football matches and you have to give them something that gets them back in."*

Those were the days. Would they ever come back again?

Supporters on the *Green Room II* were mainly upbeat about the plans:

*I'm over the moon about this, because it sets out an aim and a commitment until the target is achieved. I have always believed if the club were to give GJ a helping hand with off-pitch stuff we'd see improvement, and that the very act of striving towards attacking attendance issues in a serious way can by itself contribute to improvement because it sends an enthusiastic and unifying message.* (Cruncher)

~~~~~~~

*Good to see an acceptance from the club they need to be more pro-active. I know from my own son how getting them young can create a long term passionate and committed fan.* (valetta baby)


21November. On a rainswept night (have I mentioned the rain) at Broadfield Stadium, Yeovil fought tooth and nail in a very competitive match against Crawley Town. On 89 minutes and 38 seconds a ray of light shone down on a Crawley player and he planted the ball in the back of the net. Fortunately it was their net and when the whistle blew a couple of minutes later Yeovil Town had another three points in the bag with the 1-0 win.

Whilst happy with a good win GJ was a bit fed up with what he saw as less than sporting behaviour:

*"It's great when you come away from these places with three points. I've got fifty people screaming all obscenities at me for an hour and a half, I've got their manager telling me how lucky we were, (Paolo) Di Canio said (after Saturday's game against Swindon) they should have scored eight, this fellow (Crawley manager Richie Barker) here said that we were lucky. But we had to fight them all over the place. What we can't be is shrinking violets. We can't let people say that out of disappointment, and then let them get away with it, without coming back a bit."*

*"It was significant, and it was away from home as well. Crawley have had some good results here, and you can see why they're a decent team. They've got some very experienced players in their midst, and of course they're*

*going to have chances. I thought that we were very brave in throwing ourselves in front of things. But it would have been nice for somebody to have come along and tapped me on the back and said well played."*

At least the fans were happy:
*omg...what a result !!! Well done YEOVIL !!!!*(Green Pixie)
~~~~~~~
*Great result, let's get another 3 points on Saturday*
*Only 4 points from the play-offs, League table looking very tight up there. C'mon you Glovers!* (Bruton Glover)

Next up were Carlisle at home on 24 November. Not unnaturally Carlisle refused permission for their own player, Paddy Madden, to play against them. In a way a pity, what a joy it would have been to see him knock in a hat-trick, but in a way a blessing. We didn't want them to see how good he had become and for them to take him back to Cumbria.

In order to get the match on Yeovil borrowed some of those big magic sponges from Somerset Cricket Club in order to try and mop up the excess water. I wasn't going to mention rain again but with half the County under flood water and half the population growing web feet I couldn't let it pass.

Fortunately the referee was made of hardy stuff and declared the pitch fit for action. It often goes forgotten the amount of hard work that must go into putting on a match in any conditions but on a day like that a special mention must go to the ground staff. They did a great job.

Unfortunately it was all in vain, as far as Yeovil were concerned. Carlisle, despite an horrendous journey from near the borders of Scotland, appeared the brighter and quicker and they won the game 3-1. Only Reuben Reid got on the score sheet for the Glovers.

*Ciderspace* as they always do, gave a full and 'unbiased' report of the game but they summed it up in the final paragraph: 'A lack of buzz about the performance saw a soggy end to a soggy day, and the only good news out of the game was that Yeovil remain in 12th place - a solid mid-table team, but one upon which it is becoming increasingly difficult to understand exactly which Glovers side will turn up to the game - Tuesday's battling committed side that travelled to Crawley, or the one that was a shadow of that today.'.

Gary Johnson was not overly impressed either:

*"It was more than disappointing; it was a bit embarrassing to be fair. We didn't get going. Only two groups have come out of the game with credit, and that's our ground staff for getting the game on, and Carlisle for doing all that travelling, and having problems on the way, and putting in a much stronger performance than us. So 'embarrassing' is my word. We'll win a good one*
*and then we'll lose a bad one. That's us, I'm afraid. At the moment we're proving that we've got some that are not up for it every week." ..... It's one of those embarrassing days and I'm disappointed, but some people are going to be made to work very hard in the next 10 days. Call it a get us back in the game punishment or whatever you like.*

It was that lack of consistency that was holding Yeovil back. Win a couple, lose a couple more. Players going in and out of form. It was pretty normal Yeovil stuff really. We had the players we had, at the price that we could afford because, in the main, they lack the consistency of top performers. Still could be worse. We could be Pompey supporters!

After all the Saturday, Tuesday, Saturday, Tuesday matches that had been played, without hardly a break, a failure in the F.A. Cup gave the Glovers a ten day period to re-cooperate and regroup while others played in Round 2.
The tie of the round was the first every meeting of MK Dons and Wimbledon AFC. Passions were raised and not just between the supporters of the two teams:

*Come on you Wombles! Stuff the franchise and make all decent football fans happy. We are all behind you!*(Swat)
~~~~~~~
*Fake Dons vs Real Dons in my eyes. Winkleman is a disgrace to football. Regardless of tomorrow's result, I hope the long term outcome is that the two clubs pass each other in the league going in opposite directions.*
(Badger)
Unfortunately there was no fairy tale ending for Wimbledon.

4 December saw us back on the road to Wembley as Yeovil dispatched Wycombe Wanderers 2-0. Ed Upson and Sam Foley did the business. Paddy Madden was cup-tied so didn't play. Interestingly enough he missed the vital penalty in Carlisle's shoot-out in an earlier round. We were now in the semi-final of the Southern Section.  Next up Leyton

Orient away.

It's not all fun to be a big fish in a small pond. Coventry will tell you that. Concentrating fully on efforts to return to the Championship they seemed to forget to pay the rent on the Ricoh stadium. It was only £1.1million and they were given 21 days to pay. Default could well mean leaving the Ricoh mid- season and ground sharing at Neane Park! Remember them – Rushden & Diamonds. No longer around of course so perhaps Coventry could have the ground to themselves. One snag, they'll have to get the electricity re-connected.

Now one for the Anoraks. A very rare beast appeared at Huish Park on 8 December. It came in the shape of a draw and even more unique a 0-0 draw! Let's face it GJ doesn't believe in draws. Notts County were the opponents and despite the scoreline it was an entertaining, fully committed performance from the Glovers. Dan Burn thought he had scored with a header but the referee was not so sure. You need to get them just a bit further over the line Dan. That advice may be useful to you one day. The result dropped Yeovil to 13th in the table but they had a handy ten point cushion off the relegation candidates.

GJ was upbeat despite his dislike of the 1 point. He told BBC Somerset:

*"Certainly it was one of the best 0-0 games I've been involved in. But that desire and passion that I was looking for and have been asking for, during the last few days now, was there. They're the types of games where performance matters so much. Then the results will come at the end of that. They needed to feel that work rate and that energy throughout the game. Notts County are a good side and they're going to be there or thereabouts. They've got a lot of experience, and that've had a big budget for a little while now, in the last two or three seasons and we've more than matched them."*

The fans were upbeat as well – it must be nearly Christmas!
*Green Room II*:
*Fabulous performance - once or twice we even looked a bit like the classic GJ team, with neat passing moves and incisive waves of attacking play. Luke Ayling was immense, Super Gav looked agile and tricky - al in all, the best 0-0 I've seen for a very long time!* (Unspeakable Cad)

~~~~~~~

*Agree it was the best overall team League performance this season...... All eleven starters were MOTM contenders. Keep this up and the results will come - but probably still just short of play off potential.* (Prodigal Glover)

How many of us have said "if I had a couple of million I'd like to buy Yeovil Town" Well, theoretically you could. Huish Park Stadium Partnership 2011-12 Accounts showed that the book price for the club is £1,012,889. You would even get change!.

Fifteen matches without a win, no not some nightmare you may have had, but reality for Walsall. Naturally they had hopes of ending that with the visit of Yeovil Town but they didn't. Another draw for GJ and the lads 2-2 this time. A snatched away point is always satisfying and the Glovers left it quite late being 2-0 down with 12 minutes to go. Luckily Reuben Reid and Sam Foley made it count.
Gary had been making a few ears ring in the dressing room lately and this was no exception: He told BBC Somerset:
*"The last ten minutes was (a resilient display), but we didn't get going for the first eighty minutes, and that was disappointing. The lads know that we're disappointed with that. But we've given them a few little home truths individually and collectively. They gave it a go towards the end, and we had to make a few substitutions to get us going a little bit, because not enough of them had got their mental toughness into the game, and they were playing poorly as well."*

He was also asked about the potential of getting two of our loan players back when the transfer market opens on 1January. Regarding Korey Smith he said:
*"Korey is a super player and we like him a lot. He's a good lad and we have Yeovilified him, and he's happy with us. He's got to go back and talk about his future at Norwich. They've got to work out what they're going to do with him. So until then, we won't really know what the options are. I know that he would certainly be happy to come back to us on January 1st, and we'd be very happy to have him."*
Joe Edwards was the other player mentioned and Gary, agreeing that his contract expires in summer 2013 and the fact he had not played for Bristol City since April, would not be drawn on the possibility of actually signing him up.

The question was put quite bluntly on the Forum:

*Are we not a bit screwed?*
*Now that Edwards and Smith's loans are up and we have a busy xmas period without two players who have been vital for us.* (puffpaddy)

Some fans on the *Green Room II* had decided to form a bit of an appreciation society:
(Gary Johnson) *Worked miracles with a bottom 3/5 Lg 1 Budget.*
*Sure he reads forum so good on you Gary.*
*After 2/3 years of relegation struggle and lets be honest,dire football, we are scoring goals and trying to attack/play football.*
*From his comments support from board/various departments is not all it could be but I enjoy watching us play football again.*
*Keep it up GJ and don't lose faith.*
*Come on you Glovers.* (valetta baby)

*Couldn't agree more. Love the passion of the man, will we ever get a manager more passionate for YTFC - I don't think so. I could listen to his interviews all day long as he says it exactly as it is. Always has time for the fans and makes sure that the players follow his example. I would love someone to come along and offer him something to keep him here, because I think he would have us in the Championship, without doubt, within two years.Top man!* (garyjohn) (That's not you in disguise is it GJ?)

*Gary and Yeovil are simply meant to be together.*
*He seems at his happiest here and to most of us he`ll always be a legend. Sometime in the future we`ll look back at these as the golden years at the club so here's to the Board doing the right thing and convincing him to commit to a long term contract.....* (Brizzol Glover)
~~~~~~~
*Yeovil fans fall in to two camps: those that admire and appreciate the mighty GJ and all he does, and those that are idiots.*
*Enough said.* (Unspeakable Cad)
~~~~~~~
Wow all this outpouring of love and affection. Will it be the same after Christmas? There was not too much love and affection towards some of the players from GJ when he spoke to BBC Somerset on 20 December:
"*We're reviewing everybody's contracts. We're reviewing whether we think we're having to work too hard with some of them to get them to the level that we think that they should be at. We do feel that we need to improve the squad in quality, slightly, and improve the squad in numbers. We need to get*

*that competition, and that's what helps you get that competitiveness every week."*

Did that mean no turkey for some as they put a new C.V. together?

Some people don't half panic easily. News came through that Mark MacGhee had been fired by Bristol Rovers. Immediately the wires were humming with thoughts that GJ may go there. Get a life. No chance. And before we knew it John Ward had taken the hot seat. All was well! Christmas is a time for giving and through the post came a nice Xmas card from Santa Fry at Huish Pole. Not only that but also vouchers. A nice little gesture which was much appreciated:

*Well done YTFC on the card with the vouchers (not likely to use KFC one though - Please can we have one for Palmers!), the free London travel (although unfortunately doubt I'll be able to make it myself), and Kids for £1 on Saturday. All great gestures. Hope Santa is at HP with a big bag of Quality Street on Saturday........ Keep it up please !* (Green Haze)

~~~~~~~

*All really good stuff from the club. These things make you proud to be a YTFC. Yeovil till I die!* (garyjohn)
(Yeovil till I die! – I think I may have copyright on that!!)

Do you remember when you were a kid and you went to the local Rec. for a kick around. Someone would always turn up with a kid you didn't know and ask if "my friend can have a game?" You didn't want to choose him for your side because, well he might turn out to be a duffer. Yea of little faith. Just as well GJ was not like you. Paddy Madden's got this friend who would like a game. Kevin Dawson, out of contract from Shelbourne in the Republic of Ireland didn't even bring his own ball and yet Gary is going to take him on it seems as soon as the transfer market opens.

Last game before Christmas and Yeovil were in no mood to hand out any presents to Oldham Athletic at Huish Park. The game was played in terrible conditions (must have been that rain again) but Yeovil seemed to relish the challenge and perhaps a few of the players were fearing that exit sign that was hanging over some of them. 4-1 was the final score but the real story was a magic moment from Gavin Williams. *Ciderspace* described the occasion: 'Midfielder Gavin Williams has always been a mercurial talent over his years in football, producing moments of magic

92

that have been punctuated by his injury record. The 2012-13 season has seen frustration as a calf muscle problem has stopped him from producing any of his old magic, but 44 minutes into the match, he became Super Gav in a way not seen by Glovers fans for a few years. Marek Stech's goal kick was touched on by the Welshman in a move that took him past his marker and gave him the acceleration to bomb through the Oldham half. A defender's leg tried to take him out, perhaps realising the danger, but he managed to stay on his feet and continue his run. Then came the finish - a bullet into the top corner from 30 yards out to complete one of the best goals he's scored in a Yeovil shirt, giving Latics keeper Dean Bouzanis not a hope of getting near it. 2-1 up at half time and a real spot of quality to light up a gloomy afternoon.'

This is what it is all for. That moment when your heart sings, your body takes off and leaps around uncontrollably, that adrenalin rush, the animal noise in your throat.  Football is beautiful!!

James Hayter and Paddy Madden weighed in with a goal apiece to add to the penalty that Super Gav had already put away. What a great afternoon. Praise swiftly came from the Gaffer for his old pal:
"*Gavin was playing well even before his second goal, but he went and beat a couple of players and it all opened up like the Red Sea. He hit it with real venom and it went right into the top corner - it was a fantastic goal and something like that lifts players, management, supporters and directors. We all went up as one. It's got to be goal of the season.*"

Supporters of course loved it:
*Brilliant game, we were on top for most of it even b4 they scored after 3 mins. Super Gav best game since his return by a mile and Paddy Madden had a great game too. Atmosphere was good and a standing ovation for super Gav what a goal, looking forward to football show tonigh.t*
(yeoviltrue47*)*

~~~~~~~

But maybe a case of sour grapes from the Big Club Up The Road:
*Been sent this from a mate. It is from the Bristol City forum about Gavin Williams.*
"*He may look brilliant playing for Yeovil but take a look at who they are playing.*"
*Be careful, you could also be playing these teams next season.*
(Jimmer_YTFC.net)        What Bristol City? – no chance!

Boxing Day and Yeovil's seasonal generosity knows no bounds as the travelled to the South Coast and a gave a gift wrapped three points to Bournemouth. No point in making excuses for the 3-0 defeat but we were missing Sam Foley, who for a player making his debut in the Football League, had made quite an impact for the team. We had also lost Joe Edwards back to Bristol City and Korey Smith to Norwich after their loan period. Truth was we weren't as good as them and they were on a 14 game unbeaten run. *Ciderspace* summed it all up at the end of their match report:....'there was a gulf in class throughout the 90 minutes, and that is the gap that will currently separate genuine play-off contenders like Bournemouth, from realistically mid-table sides like Yeovil.'

It seemed that GJ was fully aware of the problems and was itching for the January transfer market to open.                    *You're crossing your fingers a little bit at this stage of the season, because you know the ones that are good enough, and you know the ones who are not good enough. Yet you have to keep them involved at the moment, because of our injuries and all of that sort of stuff."*        *"There will be some personnel changes here when the transfer window opens and some of the guys aren't up to it and are going to be shipped out. No names, but they know who they are. I'm playing people who I don't really want to. I've got a hit-list of players I'd like to bring in, but in the meantime, we've got to work very hard in the next couple of days to get things back on keel for our next game against Portsmouth."*

On*Green Room II* too much turkey had made some of them a bit fractious: *We can forget about the playoffs. We are nowhere near good enough. Today we played against a team who are there or thereabouts and the gulf in class was very evident. Faced with a good side, Yeovil cannot defend for toffee and GJ needs to dip into the transfer market and sign at least two defenders even if they are loan signings. I hope it's possible to get Joe Edwards back.* (Wurzel)

~~~~~~~

*And it's not just one game. We are poor against the teams above us and are definitely nowhere near a playoff side.* (livingthedream)

Come on guys! 'Achieve by Unity'

# CHAPTER 8

# ON A ROLL

One game to go in 2012 and as we looked back on just over half of the season, played 24, 33 points, 12th place, everyone could be forgiven for thinking that if things ran on like this we would end up in a comfortable mid table place. No one was talking about relegation for a change, but then not many were talking about play-offs either. All rather average, warm and fuzzy but hey, who wouldn't have taken that at the start of the season?

The last match then of the year, 29 December and a question mark hung over whether it would be played or not. Yeovil's first ever visit to Fratton Park was being threatened by a little precipitation. A pitch inspection however revealed enough grass amongst the puddles to allow the game to proceed. Some supporters thought it might have been good to have had a rest, but others thought now was the time to hit Pompey whilst they were in such turmoil on and off the pitch.

And so it transpired. Yeovil bounced back from the Bournemouth flop, with Dominic Blizzard and Byron Webster grabbing the goals as the Glovers snatched a 2-1 victory sending 785 fans home very happy.

GJ was also very happy:

......*But it was a great win for us, coming to Portsmouth in what was our first time at Portsmouth. So that was nice for our fans, to come to what is a very big club. At the end of the day, <u>little old Yeovil</u> has come here and turned them over, and that's really nice."*

'Little Old Yeovil' has a nice ring about it. It just about sums us up really. All the supposedly 'big' clubs, many of whom think they have a God given right to promotion from this lowly league, seem to have a condescending attitude towards us and are amazed if they can't beat us out of sight. From time to time Little Old Yeovil get in their face and embarrass the hell out of them. Wonder if we'll hear that phrase used again?

With just a couple of days left before the January transfer merry go round began, question marks hung over several players that Yeovil wanted to keep. GJ was hoping to get new loan deals on Joe Edwards and Korey

Smith. He also had his fingers crossed that Fulham would see their way to extending the loan for Dan Burn. He had been growing in stature, game by game ( that's why he's well over six foot now!) and we needed his big presence for the rest of the season. There was also the little matter of Paddy Madden. Officially set to return to Carlisle if something was not sorted soon. Gary Johnson was obviously pretty sure that he had got it in the bag when he spoke to BBC Somerset:

*With Paddy Madden, I don't know when it's officially going to come out, but I don't see him as a problem at all. I'm sure he'll be our player*

I may have said this before but just like waiting for a bus to come along, all of a sudden there are three turning up. So it was with our win against Portsmouth. However this was not just like three buses turning up but in this case a whole Bus Depot. The Pompey game started off a run of eight league wins on the trot. Eight beautiful wins, 24 fantastic points, taking us from 12th to 3rd place by 16 February.

We walloped Leyton Orient 3-0 at Huish Park to start 2013 in the best possible way. James Hayter was on target and Two goals for Paddy, who it was announced after the game had become a permanent Glover, signing a two and half year deal for an undisclosed fee, thought to have been in the region of £15 -£20,000. Peanuts for a striker who had scored nine goals in sixteen loan appearances! Paddy told BBC Somerset the day after:

*"Yes, I'm buzzing. As I've said before after my first game, Gary gave me my chance. He had faith in me and brought me down here and gave me my chance to play, get me games and play football. I'm just returning the favour for him. I've loved it since Day One down here. All the fans and everyone around the club have made me feel welcome, so I'm buzzing to be here on a permanent basis."*

And it got better! Dan Burn's youth loan was extended until the end of the season with the agreement of a further extension should Yeovil be involved in the play-offs. That'd be nice. Gary true to his word also obtained the signature of Kevin Dawson on a contract until the end of the season. He had after all shown he had what it took to play at League One level.

The only one who was not completely happy about all things Huish Park was ex Yeovil manager and now Orient's, Russell Slade:

*"It's the worst surface I've seen in League One for years, it's poor, but fair play to Yeovil because they adapted to it. I don't think we set our stall out*

*well enough in the early stages and they started as the better side and adapted to the conditions better than us.*

So it was the good old pitch that done for 'em. You should have known all about that Russ.

Fans on the Forum were pretty content with the performances so far:
*Great job by GJ and the players this year.A very Happy new year!* (pager)
~~~~~~~
*Really enjoyed today's match! Great performance by whole squad and excellent work rate considering the amount of games over Xmas. Fantastic 2 goals by Madden, his finishing today was superb...great news that he has signed with us*
*3 wins out of 4 over the Xmas period is brilliant and only 3 points off the playoffs. Up the Glovers!* (Bruton Glover)

GJ had his eyes set on another prize when he spoke after the game:
*"We're not going to rest on our laurels but we thoroughly deserved the three points. Next Tuesday's Johnstone's Paint Trophy area semi-final (against Leyton Orient) is a huge game, but it will be a different kettle of fish. It's massive to this club and we are desperate to win the trophy."*

This Cup game was our way to Wembley and in order to try and maximise the support that the '12th man' could generate, the Club agreed to pay for up to 500 supporters to travel to East London on Tuesday 8 January. Someone had filed away the memory of the Fleetwood fans free trip to Huish last season. It was certainly a very much appreciated gesture.

Unfortunately it didn't quite do the trick. Yeovil were dumped out of the Cup at Brisbane Road, with just the one goal coming in the 90th minute for the 'O's. No trip to Wembley for us then this season.
The Gaffer was none too pleased:
*"We have to say that we didn't do very well on the day. Our supporters did a lot better than us. The whole game was a poor game, and nobody can be proud of that - neither team. But they got themselves through. We've got a lot to do. We've got a bit of soul-searching to do, because unfortunately we had a few who didn't turn up. I don't think they mean not to turn up, but we certainly didn't play anywhere near how we've been playing in the last couple of weeks."*

Supporters were not unnaturally gutted. Little did they know that Yeovil's rocket had in fact blasted off and six straight wins would now follow.

Talking of rockets, fireworks were certainly seen in Preston Road a couple of nights before when The Bell burned down. A popular place for fans to gather before games, they might have to transfer their allegiance to the Huish Park marquee. Still it wasn't all bad – Mathew Dolan, a midfielder from Middlesbrough came in on loan, having turned down his home club, Hartlepool. We were certainly acquiring pulling power! One player who looked to be on his way out was Keanu Marsh-Brown. Talent yes, speed yes but somehow never put the two together to deliver a decent performance. Another one in a similar mould was Rueben Reid who also had a question mark hanging over his head. GJ was giving hints that he had something up his sleeve and that at least one new face would be arriving before the end of the transfer window.

Putting the disappointment of the JPTrophy behind them Yeovil marched north to Yorkshire on 12 January where 20,000 Sheffield United fans gathered at Bramall Lane. It turned out that they had only "come to see Yeovil, you've only come to see Yeovil". Sorry, getting carried away there. But who wouldn't have. The boys turned on the style and with Paddy Madden scoring both goals in the 2-0 win Yeovil stood in 8th place, ONE point behind the play-offs!! This was the mighty 3rd placed Sheffield Utd that we had just beaten. Yes they are a league one team on the pitch but still a huge club off it with all the resources they could want behind them. Some of their players are household names and their wages must be enormous compered to our lads. The bottom line though is that 'Little Old Yeovil' (there's that description again) have just thrashed The Blades. A very happy GJ said in interview:

*"I thought it was a fantastic performance. It was a colossal performance from our back players - a real clever, strong-running performance by our midfield four and our front two worked their socks off. Paddy's never-say-die running got us the two goals and we had chances in the first-half."*

No half measures from Yeovil fans either. The praise was being heaped on them on the Forum with these posts being typical:

*......I have to say that that is the greatest Yeovil Town performance I've ever seen. We dominated the 'best team in the division' from start to finish, won every second ball, pressed hard up the pitch, putting them under lots of pressure and were generally calm and collected. (will_ran)*

*~~~~~~~*

*We have gone there in front of 20,000 and silenced them. This is a club that is much, much bigger than us with a much bigger budget. This is the type of result and performance that will start to bring the crowds back to HP more than any run in the mickey mouse JPT.*

*Madden superb again...what can I say? Brilliant find and Carlisle must be tearing their hair out.* (wurzel)

And on the subject of a certain Mr P. Madden, ex of Carlisle, scorer of 11 goals for Yeovil and 3<sup>rd</sup> in the league one goal scorers table:

*Unbelievable Signing!*

*GJ deserves so much credit for pulling of this transfer as do the board! Can't remember the last time when we had a prolific striker who was ours and not a loanee?!*

*I hope Paddy keeps it up and fires us up the league!*

*Up the Glovers!!!!!* (Cammy)

*~~~~~~~*

*I bet the Carlisle chairman is now crying over his tea.* (glover-tom)

*~~~~~~~*

*Agree let's enjoy a great result! Be safe in the knowledge that both Marek and Paddy will be with us next year, and if they aren't we won't sell them cheap. Got to love the new longer contracts the board are offering due to Gary. Take note JF, look at the rewards of faith in our manager.* (Old Green Eyes)

We had a whole week to wait to see the heroic team run out at Huish Park against another big old club, Preston North End. The weather decided to make us wait a whole lot longer. Heavy snow forced the PNE game to be postponed and it wasn't until 29 January that Yeovil were able to play again. This time at home to MK Dons, the Club with no history and no right to respect.

In between Bristol City had sacked Derek McInnes following a 0-4 defeat at Ashton Gate which left them bumping along at the foot of the Championship. The old fears began to surface again that GJ would once again go back to them. But what about that old saying of never going back to a former club, that should protect us.....hang on. All but those of a very nervous disposition honestly believed that Gary Johnson was secure and contented in the job at Huish, knowing that things were beginning to bubble nicely and that he was going in the direction that he wanted.

Just to settle those with the jitters Gary announced:

*"I'm going to talk to the board on Monday. We're just going to have a chat with one or two players that I would still like to bring in. The squad is still small. We'll have to wait and see. Sometimes you have to move players out before you can move players in. They'll have had smiles on their faces anyway on the Saturday. So as long as they have a good Sunday lunch, then they might still be smiling on Monday!"*

There you are, totally focused on the job in hand. And just to confirm that Bristol City were not in his thoughts he went and bought Joe Edwards from them. Just about every supporter was delighted with this news. What were City thinking of. They would surely need a good player like him when they played in League One next season! And anyway City had appointed Sean O'Driscoll to the hot seat.

24 January saw Lewis Young back in training, four months after being stretchered off against Portsmouth. Welcome news as Yeovil would need all hands on deck for the busy months ahead.

On 25 January Reuben Reid left the building, joining Plymouth Argyle on loan. Even before the revolving door had stopped spinning, Keanu Marsh-Brown had followed him out, contract cancelled by mutual consent. If you don't do it the Gary Johnson way you have to go.

There was a realisation beginning to dawn on a lot of people in Yeovil that perhaps we were not just a middle of the table outfit that would see out the rest of the season with little excitement. All of a sudden the fans were beginning to look upwards and getting the feeling that maybe, we just might, just a little might, get up there in the mix for the play-offs. Fans had of course been talking about play-offs since the season began but mostly it was with tongue in cheek. Now the tongue was out and blowing raspberries at the promotion candidates above them.

Why then did Yeovil have grounds for this guarded optimism? On 19 January Doncaster Rovers and Tranmere Rovers were seven points clear of Swindon Town, Sheffield United and Brentford, who in turn were five points clear of MK Dons in sixth and last place for the play-offs. Some eight teams including Bournemouth, Walsall and Yeovil were a further three points behind. So, a lot of teams with all to play for in the next few months.

Which ones would hold their nerve? Possibly not super confident Swindon. Just like a duck looking calm on top of the water and legs flapping around underneath, so the Robins who thought they could walk it this season began to implode. Massive overspending by Paolo Di Canio became a factor in the board's resignation and the new one announced no more money for the January transfer window. Administration was in the air and also a fair few Italian expletives! Di Canio was on the wobble.

At last 29 January arrived and so did the Fancy Dons. The referee was a little unhappy about certain boating lakes that were beginning to appear on the pitch before kick-off but heroic efforts by Yeovil's ground staff allowed the game to go ahead. Thank goodness it did. 2-1 to the Town. Two more goals for Paddy (for those that were counting, six in three games since signing the contract).

There was no improvement on crowd numbers, only 3152, despite the Clubs recent offer of the last nine home games for the price of seven as part of the target 5000 initiative.

A second half off the ball incident with Paddy Madden, saw Antony Kay sent off and triggered some volatile remarks after the game from Franchise United's manager Karl Robinson. He branded Paddy as a cheat when assaulted by the innocent Kay. Fortunately for him they had *"some fantastic video footage of the incident"* and an appeal would surely succeed. Wrong! A four match ban was the only thing to succeed and another red card for Kay later in the season. He even had a go at our pitch for being a shambles. Bloody cheek! Still as the manager of the *"best team in the League – bar none "* he would know a bad pitch wouldn't he.

Turning back to ourselves we were now in seventh place, three points off the play-offs. Scary or what?

GJ was like a dog with two tails when in interview afterwards he used his own metaphor to describe the situation:
*We knew that if it could go ahead and we got a positive result, we would find ourselves like a cat amongst the pigeons in the top seven or eight. We're getting closer to where we want to be."*

Forum users purred on the internet:

*Superb game tonight. Gary Johnson is an absolute legend! So glad he came back.*
*Loving YTFC at the moment, that's 5 wins out of 6 games now!*
*Pompey, Sheffield Utd. and now MK Scum........I'm in dreamland!* (Bruton Glover)

~~~~~~~

*Out passed, out muscled, out hustled, outclassed, OUTPLAYED all over the pitch, we were just better and wanted it more.*
*This team works it collective backside off for each other.* (Das Boot)

~~~~~~~

*Fantastic win tonight.*
*This gives platform for a MASSIVE game on Saturday versus Brentford.*
*I appeal to you.*
*Come along*
*Sing your hearts out*
*Bring a friend*
*Pack the park*
*Get behind the boys...*
*and if we can get three points, we are seriously in the mix for the play-offs.*
*Who's with me!?* (greenbean11)

Yeovil reached the 31 January transfer market deadline without any further signings but announced an extended loan period for Matthew Dolan. Bring on the Brentford!

A minor problem arose just before the clash with the Bees on 2 February. There was a 'would he', 'wouldn't he' play moment with Marek Stech. Not because of injury or possible suspension but because his partner was expecting to deliver their first child at any moment. Fortunately all was quiet on the maternity front on the Saturday afternoon and just as well because Marek was extremely busy in the early stages. It all settled down in the 34 minute when Paddy Madden delicately chipped the keeper to turn things in Yeovil's favour. Playing his 100th game for Yeovil Ed Upson was not going to be upstaged and slammed in a 30 yard strike. This was then followed by a volley from Dan Burn. 3-0 and flying.
Despite this great run of form, only 4106 (including 613 Brentford fans) were lucky enough to witness the game.

The gaffer said afterwards:

*"It was a very important win over a very good side. They are above us in the table and we needed to pull them back towards us. It's a great victory and this team seems to be getting better and stronger. The nice thing is that our supporters have now started to believe that we are up there in the mix for the play-offs. Every game we go into, I am confident in this group of lads and know they're going to compete and show the desire needed to be in the mix. I feel we are on the verge of something special. I've been saying it for a while - so I'm either a witch or a good judge."*
I reckon a witch. He's certainly using his magic!

The spell was having an influence over the *Green Room II* posters:
*Watched my beloved Yeovil town smash three in against a club who have just taken a premiership side to a replay in the Fa Cup.* (Chelsea)
*The atmosphere was divine, the players were fantastic, and Gary Johnson is king (win lose or draw)*
*Week in and out I go home an away and have seen some crap over the last few years, an yes we're on the verge of something here, so I'm sure as fans we deserve some luck after all, and where we are in the league now is sublime.*
*Anyone who wants to moan about the board on your 'big' walkout please do so, but you're missing what could be history in the making here!*(ytfcwattsy)

~~~~~~~

*Congratulations to Ed Upson for winning the goal of the day on Sky Sports. It was a screamer wasn't it!* (PAT C)

Things must be going well. There is even praise for the beer tent:
*Got to the ground early today so wandered into the tent for a swift one. Busy at the bar but there were 5 young people working really hard, cheerful, efficient and I was provided with three pints in no time at all. Lively atmosphere in there too. One Brentford fan on their forum commented that the pasty and pint in the tent before the game was the highlight of his day! (Chortle)*
*I post this only because I have read many negative comments on here in the past and feel it is worth praising when it's due.*(dulverton_exile)

~~~~~~~

*Excellent comment about the Tent. When I arrived they were struggling with three staff but they got reinforcements and soon sorted it. All the staff pleasant and extremely polite. Well done!!! I have been critical of the Tent in the past but credit should be given where credit is due. Good start to a great day out.* (sparkfordunited)

Another trip up North awaited the Glovers on Tuesday night, 5th February. Possibly not the best time of the year to visit Boundary Park, Oldham which is situated 509 feet up in the Pennines. It was not nicknamed 'Ice Station Zebra' for nothing! News arrived three days before, that manager, Paul Dickov, who had seen them through a tremendous F.A.Cup run but were languishing in 20th place in the league, decided to step aside for the good of the Club. Perhaps it was a good time to play them after all. Wonder who their next manager might be?

Just when the Club were congratulating themselves on securing the loan deal with Matthew Dolan he had to return to Middlesbrough with his foot in a padded boot for extensive treatment following an injury against Brentford. When would we see him again?

Another question mark still hung over the Stech household. When was that baby going to arrive? The team, minus Stech travelled up to Oldham on 4th February. The cunning plan was for Gareth Stewart, the goal keeper coach to drive Marek up to Lancashire on the morning of the match if all was well but if the baby arrived, Gareth would travel up alone and play.

All the best laid plans of mice and men! (I thought a little Shakespeare wouldn't go amiss). Nature naturally took a hand and dumped a whole load of snow on the pitch and Yeovil Town were on their way back down the motorway before you could say icicle.

A somewhat shorter journey for the next encounter with Coventry City at the Ricoh Stadium. Yes the Sky Blues had managed to stave off eviction for non-payment of the rent and so for Yeovil fans, the opportunity to visit a quality arena.

For Marek Stech the same plan was in place as before. GJ discussed the situation on BBC Somerset:
*"I'm hoping that the 'stork' only works on Thursdays and Fridays, and that the baby arrives before the weekend. With Marek, we'll leave him at home until the morning of the game, then if he's got a few hours to spare, he'll drive up and play in the game. So we've got it sussed a little bit, in that we know when and how to bring him up and look after him, and get him back quickly as well."*

He also talked about the versatile Joe Edwards who was going to take the place of the injured Dolan:

*"His best position is the position that I need him in the most! We know that he can play right-back, left-back, centre of midfield, he can play wide on either side and I'm sure he could play in goal if you asked him to! But he's going to be playing in the centre of midfield, and that's the position right now that he's got to excel at, because that's the one that we need him in."*

It's always good to have a player like that. Remember Roy OBrien from our Conference winning team. He could play anywhere and always gave a good performance.

727 fans enjoyed both the facilities and the football at the Ricoh. They watched as just before half time Sam Foley slipped a great pass through to Paddy Madden who slotted his 15th goal into the back of the net. At the other end Marek Stech was thankfully there making important saves and keeping a clean sheet in the 0-1 win.

We had now completed six of the best, win after win after win. Heaven was Green and White! However, we hadn't quite broken into the play-off slot, we had to keep winning! The expectations of everyone were rising by the minute. Alistair Durden of BBC Bristol was even asking Gary about 'automatic promotion' GJ replied:

*You're not happy with the play-offs now? Bloody hell, what kind of a chance have I got? It will be Europe next, won't it? I don't even think we're even quite in the play-offs yet, are we?*

In praising the whole team and the 12th man he said:

*You talk about team-mates you can trust and they were out there today. They're showing signs of absolute desire and 100 percent commitment to the cause. That's what we've asked for and they've certainly been giving it. So have our supporters up the other end - they were magnificent as well and they've seen their team pick up another three away points.*
Someone on the forum could not contain themselves:
*Yes..Yes..Yes..Yes...YESS....Yess...Yessss...YEEEESSSSS!!!!!*
*Orgasmic result..AND Form...xxxx "Hey Gary Johnson "....I love that "West Country Cockney " x* (Green Pixie)

However someone else more a little more grounded:
*I think I can quite comfortably say we are safe this year. Favourites to go down! HA HA!* (GJ is God)


12 February and it was Preston North End's turn to play on the hallowed Huish Park turf. Graham Westley was bringing a team that had won only once since November and had slipped to 17th in the league. Surely we were looking at our seventh win on the trot? Yeovil were 0-1 down until the 73rd minute. James Hayter received the ball from his strike partner, Paddy Madden and Yeovil were back on level terms. 7 minutes later and Nathan Ralph sent the 3661 faithful into raptures when he smacked the ball into the roof of the net for his first Yeovil goal.  The ground went mad on 90 minutes when, guess who? raced clear and slotted past the keeper. "There's only one Paddy Madden" was sung around the ground.  Another popular chant that got everybody going was "Sacked in the Morning, you're gonna be sacked in the morning" And he was, Graham Westley walked the plank the very next day.  Wow, people power!! A Yeovil Town record of seven consecutive wins had been equalled. Even the marquee felt like the scene from 'A Thousand and One Nights' in an exotic Bedouin tent, as fans toasted the mighty Glovers in Cider and Lager.
Some fans were beginning to smell a whiff of success in the air:
*The last time I can remember being this excited was that famous night in Nottingham. We could be on the edge of history here, couldn't be more proud.* (Fortresshuish_19)
~~~~~~~
*Often a team on a good run at the end of the season wins the play off final ......* (Oracle)
GJ was keeping his feet on the ground when interviewed after the match and was not in the least bit worried that we had not got into the play-off places even after 7 wins on the bounce. He wanted to praise his players:
*we're proud of them - the workrate that you have to put in out there is unbelievable to win games.*
and highlighted his two comeback kids, Lewis Young and Nathan Ralph:
*Those two need to stand up and take a bow, because they've worked very hard over the last few months.*


St Valentine's Day and Lyla Victoria Stech made her bow. Good girl, not a game missed by Daddy! Congratulations poured in for Marek and his partner Louise.

As often when there is good news there is also sad, in this case the announcement of the death of Ken Jones, Welsh International goalkeeper who played 168 consecutive appearances for Yeovil between 1967 -1970 and also Glyn Davies, player manager between 1964 -1965.

That's life for you, we step on the conveyor belt at birth and step off somewhere further along the line. All we can do is enjoy the experience as much as we can. I guess being a Yeovil fan helps.

Coventry City received another ultimatum from the owners of the Ricoh Stadium:

*"pay up or sell up and get out of Coventry."*

Their manager Mark Robins appeared to take it literally and got himself out of Coventry. He rushed over to safer ground in Huddersfield.

Fortunately for us Gary Johnson failed to become Manager of the Month for January, that kiss of death going to Dean Smith of Walsall. But what Gary had achieved was second place in the Manager's League ratings. Only a relative unknown called Sir Alex Ferguson pipped him to first place. This really does show what a quality man we have at the helm. I've said it before but it needs saying again. A big, big thank you to those who persuaded GJ to come back.

On the evening of Friday 15 February Tranmere Rovers lost 0-2 to Shrewsbury. They were now in third place, two points above Yeovil. With both Brentford and Swindon not playing on the Saturday, a point or points would see us break into the top six. Hold onto your hat!

Our opponents at Huish Park were Scunthorpe United, who were languishing in 17th place but had won their last three games. It was all to play for.

4163 watched Yeovil romp to a 3-0 win with Byron Webster powering in a header, James Hayter with a penalty and Paddy Madden getting his 18th goal of the season.

Eight wins in succession, a new Yeovil Town record. Could this go on until the end of the season. Many fans were suffering from bruises with all the pinching themselves that was going on. We had moved into third place, only one point behind the leaders, AFC Bournemouth who lost to a revitalised Preston North End.

That mad, scarf waving manager of ours, after punching the air to all sides of the ground said in interview:

"*It was another great day for us - we are in a rich vein of form. To play on a heavy pitch like that is nothing more than miraculous, so we're very proud and scored three very good goals. We deserve to be where we are in the league. When you go third then of course you must start believing that you've created a team that could challenge for promotion.*"

Commenting on the eight win record he said:

*We're trying not to make it sound or feel amazing, because we know that we've got a fantastic athletic group that are committed to the cause. I did tell them a few games ago that we have got the group, and it's up to you lot to show it and to bring it out - bring your best game out and bring our best game out. That's what they've done. They've listened, they've learned, and they're enjoying their football. Once you get to that stage where you're enjoying your football and you're in credit, then you can be bold and be as bold as you like, and that's what they were today.*

Amongst the unbridled joy and happiness on the Forum there was also a reflective mood:

*I just have to say, as a fan who went for 40 years, but sadly no longer, that GJ has to be the best thing we ever had in all those years, whatever happens next.*
*He is so charismatic, a good man who inspires all of us who saw the dark days of non-league football, he has put the club into the Football League in style and we will never forget his massive contribution to our club-I will somehow get through the next few months,*
*But whatever occurs, Gary will be the darling of all true fans of YTFC.*
*This is the most important time in our history.*(stewart.barnes)

~~~~~~~

*In amidst all the credit going to Gary for the fantastic run we're on, Terry and Darren deserve huge credit for their parts in the upturn. Gary wouldn't have come back without Terry staying on and its obvious after so long working together, the dynamic between the three of them is perfect.*
*Long may it continue.* (Oldland Glover)

Just to extend our happiness, the excitable Italian up the road at Swindle found his position to be 'untenable' and resigned. You just knew it would end in tears.

Now it was off to one of our happy hunting grounds, Doncaster Rovers. Remember when we won the Conference back in 2003 at the old Belle Vue ground? What a happy day, could we ever top that? Donny came up with us that season and here they are again looking for promotion. Any chance we could be going up together again? These were the thoughts of many as the team ran out at The Keep Moat Stadium.

It was not to be nine wins in a row, well we were getting a bit greedy after all. 1-1. The Glovers went for the smash and grab technic with Paddy scoring in the sixth minute and defending almost perfectly for the next eighty four. Just the one blip right on the stroke of half time as perhaps they were thinking about that cup of tea or whatever they have in the dressing room. It was still a good away point against the team that aspired to be Champions. The downside was that James Hayter, sore foot and Jamie McAlister, injured ankle looked doubtful for the next game only three days away at Colchester United.

The draw meant we slipped back to fifth place, it being so tight now up the top that teams were swopping places for a pass time. Bournemouth fell from first to sixth, Sheffield United jumped into the top spot and Doncaster, Brentford, Swindon and Tranmere were all milling around in the mix.

Gary Johnson said afterwards:

"*We got the goal early and we always knew Doncaster would come back at us. When you get used to winning like we have you are always disappointed when the run comes to an end. But we can't be too unhappy that we've come to one of our main promotion rivals and gone away with a point. He's in an unbelievably rich vein of form. I only wish the goal had been enough to win the game but, in fairness, it was pretty even overall.*"

Talking about how injuries and mounting bookings were affecting the small squad he gave a little insight into his thinking:

*Jamie (McAllister) was on nine bookings, and I sort of wanted him to push the referee as he walked off the pitch, so that he could get a booking and be out for two games whilst he was injured! And I couldn't get the message out to him! (laughs) But don't tell anyone that one, because that would have been clever. But anyway, it didn't happen. So unfortunately he's going to miss a couple injured.*

And by the way, following our few recent successes, (Sir) Gary Johnson had taken the number one slot in the Managers League table. Officially we had the best manager in the Country.  We all knew that anyway.

Where would you not want to be on a cold Tuesday night in February? How about the Community Stadium, Colchester in front of 2367 relegation worried supporters. It seemed that Yeovil players felt the same as for once they could not get their game together. Colchester bounced back from a 1-5 home defeat by Tranmere on the previous weekend and were comfortable winners 2-0.
Gary felt sorry for the 183 hardy souls that travelled to Essex:
*"We didn't really show any of the innovation that we show, or have shown in our good run. We huffed and puffed but we didn't get anywhere today. It's a long old way for our supporters and they've done well for us. But we didn't really give them anything today, and the players didn't give themselves anything and didn't give us anything and didn't give the supporters anything. They're disappointed in there, but we did look weak today."*

With Jamie McAllister missing the Forum were noticing a pattern:
*I may be wrong but I suspect that we have been beaten every time macca has been missing. Hope he is fit on Saturday if that is the case.* (Camberwick Green)

<p style="text-align:center">~~~~~~~</p>

*Nope, you're spot on. He's missed five games this season...all defeats!*
*v AFC Bournemouth 0-1*
*v MK Dons 0-1*
*v Leyton Orient 1-4*
*v Carlisle 1-3*
*v Colchester 0-2*  (Oldland Glover)

Anything you need to know, ask the *Green Room II* posters. With all this knowledge, passion and commitment what we couldn't do if the Club was run by a Supporters Trust? On the other hand we're not doing too bad under the present set-up. A couple of seasons back I never thought I would say that but hey I'm just a fickle football fan. Up the Glovers!!

Before the vital match at home to Tranmere Rovers Yeovil signed striker Wes Fletcher from Burnley on a month's loan but Gary was wary about bringing in any more short term loans to boost the now depleted squad *"I don't want to bring in somebody that's going to mess up the dressing room. I'm the one messing up the dressing room at the moment, I'm afraid! But they know what it's all about and hopefully we can turn them around like we've done before."*

Saturday 2 March was going to be a big test for the Glovers. Tranmere Rovers had been the high flyers all season, rarely leaving the top spot and of course they had walloped Colchester who in turn had just beaten us. With James Hayter and Jamie McAllister restored to health, well sort of, injections in the ankle to keep Jamie on two feet, Yeovil could field our strongest team.

As we might have expected the game was a hard fought close contest and it needed a spark of magic to separate the two teams. Magician Ed Upson stepped up to dip a wicked free kick into the Tranmere net and send the fans in the Thatcher's Gold Stand wild as they watched the ball thundering towards them. 1-0 then and comfortably placed in 5th.
GJ said:
*"We've had that little blip now. All teams are going to have a time when they get beaten, so we needed to bounce back. I haven't looked at the table yet, it's too early, but I know the results and they matter. There's a couple of teams having a longer blip than we have had, and we have been in a good run of form over the last 12 games. The support we're getting is growing and the fans are getting behind us. They are seeing their team giving absolutely everything."*
*Our home form has been very good for a little while now. The support is growing, and getting noisier as it grows. That's nice and they're beginning to believe that they've got a team that's going to challenge for promotion. I thought Tranmere were a very difficult team to play against, and that's what they've been all year....*
That home support was increasing, 4826 for the game and what was also increasing was the buzz of excitement around the town. Things were really taking off.
From the forum:
*Good to see that Gary's plea for supporters to get behind the team was answered...*
*A crowd of 4,826 was also buoyed by more than 300 people brought in by*

111

*the YTCST, great work from Sara, Roy and Bob there. Sitting in the Screwfix Stand, it was great to see the end block of the Main Stand so full with kids, a great sight.*
*Be nice to get to target 5k sooner rather than later, seven wins in a row will help to do the trick.* (Oldland Glover)

For those of you who cannot remember back that far, it was 2 March 1888 when a certain Mr William McGregor, secretary to Aston Villa Football Club wrote a letter to a number of select football clubs suggesting they might like to form a league. I think we should raise a glass to Mr McG. and thank him for the wonderful thing league football is. What the hell would we do on Saturday afternoons without it?

In out, in out, that's Matthew Dolan. He must have known the road between Yeovil and Middlesbrough pretty well. Once again he returned home for treatment, this time with a groin injury. It was a great pity as he had showed, on the rare occasions that he has played, that he fitted in well with the Yeovil set-up. Would he take the scenic route back to Huish Park again for a third time we wondered.

You could have written a book about the toing's and froing's at Portsmouth F.C. There was more activity going on in the High Court than on the pitch at Fratton Park. The upshot appeared to be that the Portsmouth Supporters Trust had come out on top in the battle to control the club. Well there's no doubt that they will make a better job of it than some of the charlatans in the past. Wouldn't it be great if football could be swept clean of much of the rubbish that runs it? What would Mr McGregor say?

We were able to take a breather on the following Tuesday 5 March. Others however could not. Donny were away at MK Dons and Brentford at Stevenage. The forum was awash with posters struggling with their deep seated dislike for the Franchise club but the need to put that aside and hope for them to beat Doncaster. Similarly, Stevenage, not everybody's favourite team could do us a favour. They both did and we rose to 4th place without kicking a ball. That's the way to do it!

Other posters were turning their attention to the future:

*At this moment in time would you take...*
*-A Wembley play-off final which would mean 90 minutes away from*
*Championship football?*
*Or do you believe we could really achieve higher i.e. an automatic*
*promotion spot?*
*Looking at our run in to the end, I don't see why we couldn't be serious*
*contenders for an automatic place. As long as we maintain a fully fit*
*starting 11 and madden keeps his shooting boots on?* (GreenAndWhite)

~~~~~~~

*No reason for us not to get the automatic promotion places as I mentioned*
*in a previous topic yesterday, but can you imagine the feeling we would all*
*have if we were able to win at Wembley and get Promoted? It would be the*
*greatest feeling I feel and I know it would be amazing to finish top two but I*
*don't think anything else would compare to a play-off final victory.*
(Tommyboy)

~~~~~~~

*Never thought that it would be this good, didn't dare to.... brings goose*
*bumps just thinking about the next game....*
*We're gonna do it I'm sure of it, we're gonna do it...... I'M SO EXCITED!!!!!!!!!!*
(CKIN YEOVIL)
Saturday 9 March and Hartlepool, jewel of the North Sea Coast, beckoned.
Relegation candidates, fighting for their survival are not the best of teams
to meet and so perhaps the 0-0 draw that resulted was not so bad.
*Ciderspace* reported:

*...Goalless it stayed, and a result that probably didn't favour either team, but*
*one that the Glovers would be slightly happier with at the end, particularly*
*given incoming news that Brentford and Bournemouth had lost, with the*
*latter now having suffered five defeats in a row since topping the table. For*
*the Glovers, they drop one place to fifth, but given they have increased the*
*gap between them and the seventh placed Cherries by an additional point,*
*it's certainly not a point to be sniffed at.*

GJ, with a seven hour return journey ahead reflected:
*"It's a rare 0-0 draw for us. Both teams have a lot to play for and maybe this*
*point will look OK later in the season. Let's not hope we look back at is as*
*two dropped. Hartlepool are in decent form and they were trying to win the*
*game as well, I was just disappointed we didn't find that killer ball. It's a*
*long way for a 0-0 draw. It's a better result for us with the way other results*
*went and we are still very much in the mix."*

Gary Johnson obviously felt the need for an extension to the squad and drafted in 22year old left back, Ben Gordon, a free agent on a month's deal.

Two bad things about the up and coming fixture at home to Crawley on Tuesday12 March. The first being that there was snow in the air and how much would fall was a concern. The club put out a volunteer request to help cover he pitch. The second was that Trevor Kettle was going to be the man in black. The omens were not good but as luck would have it, the snow failed to materialise and so did Kettle. He must have been double booked that night because James Adcock held the whistle. Trouble was all our luck had been used up and The Glovers let slip a 2-0 first half advantage, secured by Byron Webster and Paddy Madden and Crawley scored twice in the second half for a 2-2.
We're cool. No sweat. A point's a point. Still in 6th.

Keep calm and carry on. Well that was the message from Chief Executive, Martyn Starnes when announcing a profit of £53,379 for the year ending 30 June 2012.

Fortunately we were at home again in the following game, a chance to get Fortress Huish back on track. Somewhat erratic Swindon were the guests. Now that Paolo had gone they were hopeful of signing up three players before the game with the Glovers. The Football League were not so keen, keeping in force a transfer embargo imposed for the Wiltshire outfit's irregularities.

If you play the game by the rules you don't get involved in embargos and the like and so Yeovil Town were able to sign two loanees before the game. Vitalijs Maksimenko, a Latvian left back and Jordan Cook, striker. The T.V. cameras were in attendance for this top of the table clash and in order to give an extra bit of colour to the night, some 3000 flags were given out to Yeovil fans.
Unfortunately there weren't many good occasions when they were able wave them. Certainly not when Marek Stech brought down a player and a penalty was awarded. 0-1 at half time and this turned into 0-2 on the stroke of full time. In addition Jamie McAllister picked up his tenth yellow card and will be missing the next couple of games. They say that every

cloud has a silver lining. Jamie can now rest that ankle and be ready for the big push.

We had reached the Target 5000 goal but this was not much consolation to Gary Johnson when he spoke to BBC Bristol:

*We mustn't let our season fade away - I'm not going to let that happen. I'll tell them home truths, which I always do, and they always know that. There's a few of them that I didn't think realised the importance of the game, or certainly didn't show that in their body language. We've got to make sure that in the next couple of games we fight back and get ourselves back in those play-offs. The second goal was a bit disappointing, but we'll fight another day, as they say.*

Supporters were weeping and there was gnashing of teeth. The great abyss awaited us. We were doomed and destined to play in purgatory. Honest it was of Biblical proportions on the forum:

*I am worrying because I can see the little spark has started to die. We don't really look a threat, the pitch is dreadful for a passing side and fear we may end up petering out with a whimper unfortunately.* (Pager)

~~~~~~~

*Players have totally lost confidence, I really thought we were second best but should have taken our chance when they came-really disappointing! Have given ourselves a lot to do if we are going to go up! They all have been must win games but Saturday is actually a MUST WIN or I think that will be the end of it for this season unless some miracle occurs* (YTFC0911)

~~~~~~~

*Thought the ref did ok but any 50/50 calls went the way of Swindon, our appeals fell on deaf ears. We were 2nd to everything tonight, the pitch is abysmal and Swindon were by far the better side. We need a reaction and quickly.*

*Again McAllister is forced off with injury and we crumble.* (Cheshire Glover)

~~~~~~~

What we needed was a bit of good old British stiff upper lip. Wait 'til you see the whites of their eyes. Gordon at Khartoum would've managed. Feel better? Let's carry on then.

News of the re-arranged fixture at Oldham comes shortly before news of their new manager filters through. It was only Lee, flipping, Johnson!!! Lee said much earlier in the season that he would never work for his father again and true to his word he would now be working against him.

Beating off around 120 applicants, Lee becomes the youngest manager in the league and his first task is to stave off relegation for the 'Latics'. I am sure every Yeovil fan wished him luck in his new role, apart from on 16 April.

A very proud Dad spoke of Lee's abilities and professionalism but with tongue in cheek he said:

*Hopefully he'll keep them in the league. Get beaten by us, but still keep them in the league! What a day that might be - any sort of scenario could be happening. If I do sell him Paddy Madden, and I play my Youth Team on that day, then you'll know that there's a bit of a father and son thing going on!"*

Back to the more serious business of getting Yeovil promoted and another hell of long journey up to the Scottish Borders and Carlisle. The English club, Berwick Rangers play in the Scottish League, couldn't Carlisle do us all a favour and do the same. There must be some way we could avoid this long arduous trip. Promotion to the Championship would be the answer. I guess we must let them off though as they gave us Paddy!

So, Spring time in Cumbria, just a light dusting of snow on the pitch at Brunton Park. 158 Yeovil Eskimos fought their way through snow drifts in the Midlands to cheer the Glovers on. This is by far and away above and beyond the call of duty and each one of them should be saluted (or certified!). In the past their efforts have been rewarded with replica shirts but that day all they craved were three precious points. Up until 90 minutes they believed that their wish would come true. Yeovil were strolling it, 3-1 up with Dawson, Madden and Hayter on the score sheet. What happened after that God only knows. Just as the board was going up to indicate 3 added minutes, Carlisle hit their second. From that point Yeovil could have kicked the ball anywhere, high into the stand, into the bloody Irish Sea, but no, on 93 minutes and 45 seconds the ball ricocheted of the unfortunate Luke Ayling into the back of the net.

For those who did not have the stamina to travel to the match, Sky T.V's Soccer Saturday brought every horrendous minute to life. Fans were spitting feathers, chewing the carpet and sobbing in disbelief. How could they let two points slip like that? How could such a team ever get promotion?

After the men in white coats had left the building GJ spoke:

*"I'm gutted. It was a dagger to the heart. We are still there or thereabouts and I've got to keep shoving and probing to get them to believe they can get there. It hurts a lot. All of a sudden players start hitting the wrong ball at the wrong time and jumping out of tackles and not winning things."*

*"I've got a massive job to keep them competitive. Some players have it and some aren't competitive enough. If you are mid table then 3-3 at Carlisle sounds not bad, but I make it a very poor result. But Paddy Madden gave a fantastic performance. He chases lost causes and goes beyond the call of duty, which is why he will have a terrific career in the game."*

*We'll keep pushing. I promise - I absolutely promise. I'll drag every ounce that we've got out of them. We'll have to see how far we can get.*

After the dust had settled on the forum keyboards, many wise old heads were urging calm. The team had not turned into a bad team overnight. They would emerge again and take us to the sunny uplands through the paths of uncertainty and the lakes of gloom. (Note to self – stop taking these peculiar tablets and just stick with the motto – 'In Gary We Trust')

*After yesterday's shock, horror, and tears, the forum last night seemed to return to positive vibes....*
*Keep that going, only 5 days 'til we have the chance to rebuild Fortress Huish walls and put Walsall where they belong...*
*KEEP KEEP KEEP THE FAITH.*(Burnham Dad)

Someone needed the anti-depressants though:

*Bottled it (again!) Won't need to worry about the play offs now, will be struggling for top ten at this rate* (Swat)

Another re-inforcement arrived on 26 March in the shape of Angelo Balanta, a winger from QPR. Wes Fletcher returned to Burnley after only sitting on the substitutes bench and Jordan Cook went home to Charlton with a knee injury.

Hoping it was third time luck, Matthew Dolan returns once more to Huish Park. We all hoped he could make it through to the end of the season this time. One thing we did not have to  worry about was Coventry City who were deducted 10 points for going into adminstration. It dropped them down to a comfortable position of 14th.

7th played 8th on Good Friday,29 March. Walsall had been on a great run and were threatening to jump into the play-offs at someones expense. Could Yeovil halt this run of four games without a win and get themselves back in contention? 5594 turned up at Huish Park to roar the Glovers on to victory. It didn't happen. Both teams cancelled each other out in a 0-0 draw. 7th we started and 7th we remained. So tantalisingly close but oh so far away.

Was the Gaffer wobbling? Speaking to BBC Somerset he said:
*"We've got to worry about our form. That's because you can have a game in hand but if your form is not quite there, then that game in hand doesn't mean anything. So we've got to work very hard and the players have got to work very hard to get their form back and to get their mental toughness back. That's what they've got to do. They can only do that themselves. It's that self-motivation, and realising how close they are and bringing out their best game. If they're going to be nervous, then they're not going to be at the next level, and they might not be at this level very long. So we're asking them to bring out their Championship form, because if they are going to go up, then they've got to be Championship level. Certainly today we didn't show that."*

No that wasn't a wobble. He was as focused as he had been from the very start and he wasn't going to be put off now.

Despite now not having won for five games and being outside the play-offs the more positive amongst us were posting their thoughts:

*Well, as I sit here dreaming of next year's Championship footie, I wondered what our play-off run in will be?*
*I reckon 6th place against Sheff Utd in 3rd, so that will be another great away night out for the 2nd leg - can we have another Forest game again please, although just not leaving it quite so late as I have higher Blood Pressure than that year!*
*Wembley next, and I reckon Swindle there, (as I think Donny and Muff are looking good for Automatic) Good day out, great game, and the winning goal from a certain Irishman!*
*That's wot I'm guessing, what do you think guys?*
*P.S no comments on not making it into top 6, that's not open for negotiation!!......Cheers.* (Burnham Dad)

<center>~~~~~~~</center>

*Sooner take on Brentford at Wembley but agree re Sheffield Utd!* (Swat)

But there's always one:
*I shouldn't worry too much...........at this rate we won't make the play-offs.*(minesapint)

To complete the Easter holiday programme on 1 April, a trip to the fine city of Nottingham was on the cards for 349 Yeovil fans. Not of course to the City Ground, the scene of one of our finest hours, 5-4 winners in the 2nd leg of the play-off semi-finals in 2007 (oh to do that sort of thing again!), but across the road to Meadow Lane.

Notts County did not have a huge amount to play for, sitting safely in mid-table, no fears of relegation or hopes of promotion. What they did have was that professional mind set of playing as hard as possible for the sake of their paying public. So no favours coming Yeovil's way. As luck would have it Yeovil had the same mind set and two goals from Paddy Madden, the ultimate poacher and third time lucky, Matthew Dolan, with a beautiful free kick, was enough to bring home the points in a 1-2 win.
A back on track Gary Johnson said later:
"*Some of the players that haven't played well in the last couple of games came up trumps. We found a few things in this game that we have been lacking recently and hopefully now we can keep doing them for the remaining games.*"
*Ciderspace* summed it up: 'On the whole, this was a deserved victory, even if Yeovil were never head and shoulders above their opponents on the day. The difficult pitch meant that this was a game largely of attrition and concentration, than one of silky ball skills, and the most vital part was of course the three points. Still five more games to go of twists'n'turns, but after today, it's firmly back in Yeovil's hands to secure the play-off place they currently hold.'

Just when we thought we had slipped through April Fool's Day without being caught, a little news item flashed up, ' Di Canio appointed Sunderland manager'
Nice one. Good try! The crazy part of course is that it was true. Good luck Sunderland.

# CHAPTER 9

# PLAY-OFF'S

The scene was set, five games to go, two at home, Shrewsbury and Crewe and three away, Stevenage, Oldham and Bury. Some teams who were in the play-off spots still had to play each other and so we could expect fireworks all round before the end.

Yeovil made a decision to completely close down the Centre of Excellence for young players. On the face of it it seemed a bit harsh but Gary explained the decision:
*"The club has worked hard to make the youth programme work but it has not been able to produce any players for the first team squad in recent years. It is harder for local lads to progress to that level now we are in League One and looking to compete at the upper end of that division. I have therefore advised the board of directors to focus the recruitment resources we do have on 18 to 21-year-olds that have not been given the opportunity of first-team football at Premier League and Championship clubs."*

On the whole fans felt this was the right move:

*Sad in a way and we could lose out on a local superstar but in today's market I can definitely see the benefit.* (baige)
~~~~~~~
*You have to look at how beneficial the youth team is to the club. How many players in the last ten years have become successful at our club coming through our youth setup? Not many (Weale, Alcock?). Are we, in a sense, throwing good money at it with no return?* (Dazz)

Moving swiftly on (about time I hear you say), we met Shrewsbury Town on 6 April.
*Ciderspace,* as always, was there to report every move of the match but the important bit was 2-1 to Yeovil. James Hayter with a penalty and Paddy with his 23rd of the season. Oh you beauties!! Third place, seven points ahead of Tranmere in seventh.

Dates for the play-offs had been announced. The Bank Holiday weekend from Friday 3 May – Monday 6 May, with the final on Sunday 19 May.

All eyes were now beginning to firmly focus on who we might meet, who we'd like to meet and who we wouldn't. Most fans didn't want face Bournemouth, let them go up automatically if necessary. Lots hoped for Donny, always our favourites, but it looked like they would be going up automatically as well. This left  Sheffield Utd, Brentford and Swindon barring a last minute surge from maybe Walsall. We did not want Swindon but Brentford would be nice in the final. Bring on the Blades then!

Forum fans were working up a steam by now:

*6 weeks from now....?*
*What might you be doing?*
*Where might you be?*
*Were might you have been for a day out?*
*How might you be feeling?*
*Still screaming....*
*In some service station with lots of fellow fans...*
*London town....*
*OMG.......*(Burnham Dad)

Just as we were thinking about Sheffield Utd they decided to sack their manager, Danny Wilson. They had just lost 0-2 to Crawley and were now in 5th place. Their expectations of automatic promotion had gone out of the window and it was obviously too much for the Board.

Either a very brave or very foolish thing to do. Time would tell!

Club Captain and all round inspiration, Jamie McAllister was back in training following his ankle injury and suspension. GJ talked about the situation to BBC Somerset:

*"It's a little bit the same as it was before (in terms of McAllister's injury). We rushed him back early, and it didn't quite work out, although I think we had a couple of good results when he came back. But now we've had a couple of results with him not being in the team, so at least it gives us that option to absolutely clear him up with his injury. So it's a little bit of a juggling act right now as to when we bring him in, and when we still have to rest him."*

As long as he's back for the play-offs, all will be well.

13 April and it's that man again! Like a bad penny Graham Westley had returned to manage Stevenage and it gave our travelling fans the opportunity of suggesting his future in the morning once again.

GJ speaking before the game described how a season was like the steering of a boat through iceberg waters. *"Often there's a lot more below the water than there is above it, especially in Stevenage's case. We'll have to manoeuvre past it."*

Thanks to the gallant crew, the good ship 'Little Old Yeovil' did just that. Sam Foley and James Hayter steered the mighty Glovers to a 0-2 win as they sailed defiantly into the play-offs. With Walsall getting a draw, Tranmere Rovers and MK Dons both losing we could not be ousted. A jubilant Gary Johnson speaking after the game said:

*"It's a magnificent achievement for our club, our supporters and our players to get into a play-off position. We've still got to keep going though and try and keep touch the teams above us. I wanted us to consolidate and we have. It's nice to do that. It's been a fantastic end to the season now whatever happens."*

*"In the first half we were absolutely hopeless. I felt most of them didn't turn up. It was 0-0 so that was the only positive. All of a sudden I must have touched a few buttons because when we came out after the break we were totally different. We looked a Championship team against a team that's hanging on in there. All of a sudden we played our football, we took our chances and scored two goals. Sam scored a lovely goal, we know he's got that in him though. James has 15 goals and that's fantastic. He scored a great goal."*

Right so GJ had got his sights still on the teams above us. Automatic promotion is what he wanted, what he really, really wanted. And who was standing in the path to this goal. Yes of course it was Lee Johnson. As the day of the match approached the media went mad. T.V, Radio, Newspaper, Bongo Drums all were reporting this phenomena of Father/Son, that tussle of family bonds, duty to club, moral fibre, and who wanted to win it most! We did of course, we needed just a couple of extra points and we might grab the automatic prize. For Oldham, safety in league one was all that was at stake. No pressure on anyone then.

Remind me what plan B was again? Oh yes, forget about the automatics and concentrate on the play-offs. Plan B it was then. Lee took the honours on 16 April at Boundary Park 1-0.

*Ciderspace*, as every super cool in the face of the mounting white heat of excitement that was just beginning to sweep us of our feet, said: 'The final

whistle was greeted by a mini pitch invasion by Oldham fans - results elsewhere meant they had pulled five points clear of the drop, although in doing so, Lee Johnson had pretty much ended his father's automatic promotion hopes. No big disaster in the cold light of day, but nonetheless a disappointment given the opportunity that was presented by this game in hand. Now gone, it's far more likely that the play-off semi-finals will represent Yeovil Town's next big match in their fixture calendar.'

A disappointed Gary Johnson when interviewed for BBC Somerset said: *We're very proud of what they've achieved. But every now and again - and you've seen it - our 'Little Boy Lost' game comes out. Unfortunately it came out today when there weren't enough of them anywhere near their individual games. There's no way that you can get a team game going if individuals are not performing.* *We're in the play-offs. We're 'Little Ole Yeovil' - we've reached for the stars, but it may - it's still open to us of course - not get there (for automatic promotion). But we've got to the play-offs, so it's going to be a fantastic end to the season, so I'm going to look forward to that.*

Asked about meeting up with Lee later: *I'll try not to talk about football, and he'll try to bring it up on a few occasions, so I'll just ignore him and talk about something else!*

We were taking our lead from Gary as most of us were in a good place about the situation. Forum posters were being sensible, forward planning and well ok a bit excited!:

*We were facing an Oldham side tonight with relegation hanging over them like the sword of Damocles. Anybody with one iota of football intelligence knows that games like this at this time of the season are the hardest you can get.*(kota kinabalu)

*What I think we and they need to focus on now is the next 5 games, cos that's all we are talking about, 450 minutes of football, with an amazing prize at the end.*
*And if we were going to be really practical, we could lose 3 of those games, yes 3!*
*Momentum is obviously vital, but there are only 2 games we have to win, and that's the one on Monday 6th May, and then 13 days later on 19th May. I cannot wait to be at every single minute of the rest of this season, and will*

*thoroughly enjoy shouting my heart out for the lads, proud of the season, and of what's to come....*(Burnham Dad)

~~~~~~~

*I'm so excited that we are in the play offs after the long wait since we were last in them. What happiness that brought to our supporters! It was one of the best days of my life experiencing that and I can't believe were reliving the memories again. I don't care who we get, either way we will have to get through whoever it will be, and to be the best we need to beat the best. It will probably make me the happiest man alive if we get to Wembley and go on to win!!*
*Here's to reliving those special times, Let's get behind the team and sell out HP! Let's make history.* (Tommyboy)

A minor catastrophe befell the club from Ashton Gate when a Forum poster wrote:
*Bristol City relegated..*
*Confirmed tonight after losing at home to Birmingham 0-1*
*Personally I think it's a shame, never had a problem with City fans who have always treated me with a darn site more respect than the Gasheads.*
*In the event of us staying in league 1 it will be a great derby with a big crowd.*
*In the event of us going up it will be mightily embarrassing for Somerset Sound having to explain why Yeovil don't have top billing on the programme...*(Wurzel)

Bad news for us as well. Dan Burn, suspended for the Oldham game for yellow card accumulations had also injured his ankle and had returned to Fulham for treatment. We all hoped that they'd have the finest medical facilities and could get him back to us ready for the big push.
20 April, the last home game of the season saw 5293 fans come to cheer on the boys and wish them well for the all important games to come. It was important to go out on a high. Crewe Alexandra would be a tough nut to crack, having just won a Wembley final of their own at the expense of Southend United in the Johnson's Paint Trophy.

Not that tough a nut, as 51 seconds into the game Joe Edwards slotted the ball into the net. That was about it for memorable action but a win is a win.

The end of season presentations were made and it seemed that Paddy Madden would need a pretty strong shelf for all that silver-ware. Congratulations also to Marek Stech, Jamie McAllister and Dan Burn.

We were almost forgetting Bury away 27 April, our focus being now on who we would get in the semi's. Bournemouth had clinched automatic and the other place would be decided at Griffin Park – Brentford –v-Doncaster Rovers. The winners would go up, the others to compete in the play-offs. You couldn't write the script. So that would definitely give us the possibility of Sheffield United, Swindon and either Brentford or Donny.  Do we really care who? We are there.

Before the journey GJ indicated that he was wrapping some players in cotton wool and would only bring them out on the big day:
."*We'll only be taking three outfield players for the bench, along with the goalkeeper. We can't afford anyone who is remotely injured to be anywhere near the game. We're giving our injured players relentless treatment - morning, noon and night - in the hope that we can put out what we hope is our best squad for the play-off games.*"

Gigg Lane, Bury,401 Yeovil fans, many in Leprechaun outfits.  3.05 pm. 1-0 down, 3.32pm. 3-0 down. Second half: 4.13pm, James Hayter, 4.45pm.Kevin Dawson. Game over. 4th place in League One. I believe I have given enough detail.

The season was over and those relegated were, Portsmouth, Hartlepool, Bury and Scunthorpe. What we were all really looking for was results from elsewhere. Swindon Town who were in fifth lost and dropped to sixth. Sheffield United who were sixth, drew and climbed to fifth. That was all we needed to know. Sheffield United were to be our opponents and for reasons relating to Sheffield Wednesday being at home on the Saturday, our 1st leg of the semi's would be on Friday 3rd May 7.45pm at Bramall Lane.

The Gaffer took heed of the defeat at Bury when speaking after the game:
*It was a really poor first half and we can't afford a half like that in the play-offs, so maybe it's a warning not to go into the play-offs complacent.*"
"*Our win at Bramall Lane earlier in the season was one of our best and we're going to need that type of performance again because it's going to be like the play-*

*off final up there. There will be 35,000 Sheffield fans getting behind their team and we've got to go up there and make sure we don't choke."*
Supporters were in Heaven with the thought that 'Little Old Yeovil' could be going up!

*Just to say to Gary, thank you so much for all you have done this season. No matter what happens in the play-offs, you have given YTFC fans some joy. To have come into such a poorly run club and been the sole impetus behind the change this season, is stunning. If we don't go up, I feel GJ will be off and the veil will fall. But well done Gary. (touched)*

There was great drama at Griffin Park where Brentford needed a win to clinch the 2nd automatic spot with Bournemouth as Champions. Doncaster needed a draw to get that 2nd place and a win to become Champions themselves if Bournemouth drew or lost. News came through as the game went well into extra time that Bournemouth had drawn. With the score on 0-0 whoever could score now would go up, there being so little time left. 94 minutes and a penalty was awarded to Brentford. Up stepped loanee, Trotta (not sure if his first name was Rodney) and smashed the ball onto the bar. From the ricochet Donny swept the ball up field and Coppinger tapped it into the net. All over – Doncaster Rovers, Champions of League One.  Brentford, gutted and in disbelief. Would they be able to come back from such an horrific experience and compose themselves enough to beat Swindon in the play-off semi?

Bournemouth came second – nobody remembers who came second, only Champions and Play-Off winners!

Wasn't that a pleasure to be able to look on in a detached way as others struggled to get a result. We could sit back and chuckle, content in the knowledge that the future was securely in our hands. All we had to do now was score one more than Sheffield and we were on our way to Wembley. Simple stuff this football!!

Did I mention as we'd gone through the season that a certain Paddy Madden has been scoring goal after goal after goal? I thought I did. The result was that he was declared the winner of the League One 'Golden Boot' for scoring 23 goals. Three also ran's managed 19 apiece. Easy peasy Paddy! (he was also included in the PFA League One Team of the Year – not bad for a Carlisle substitute).  While we are on the subject of leading scorers, credit must be given to James Hayter for his fantastic 16 goals, which in most seasons would have made him Yeovil's top scorer.

The Club had earlier announced the new Season Ticket deal for the 2013/14 season. Buy one quick and pay last season's price whether we are League One or Championship. For those with the reddies it was a must, but really the next big priority was buying other tickets. Tickets for Bramall Lane, tickets for Huish Park, tickets for coaches.

The race was on. It was the turn of all those unsung heroes from the Green & Whites, Cary Glovers, Away Travel Club and Devon & Dorset's who spring into action and organise the transport, book people on, chase the money, deal with the cancellations. Thankless work but so very important.
There was also the merchandise to sell, flags, scarves, hats, you name it. Again volunteers taking the goods to the fans and raising funds for the club:
*Flags Hat and Horns*
*Paul Hadlow from the green and white and Mark Kelly will be selling all of the above at the ground on Friday and Monday all will be sold at a good price so please do not buy things from people in the town centre and outside the ground.(Mojo)*

~~~~~~~
*Does the money raised go to the club?* (Rich_the _Glover)
~~~~~~~
*Yes Rich, green & whites and ex-ytisa all goes back to club. Don't buy from shady street sellers.* (will_ran)

For those who could not make it to Sheffield and did not have time to fix a Sky dish to the wall, the Club announced they would open the Alex Stock Bar to all comers to watch the match It's a nice gesture from the Club but wouldn't it be good if we could all socialise together more often.

*Ciderspace* gave us a blow by blow account of every play-off game that Sheffield United had been involved in but then summed it up in a paragraph: 'Friday night's fixture will therefore be Sheffield United's seventh attempt to win the divisional play-offs. The defeats in 1997, 2003, 2009 and 2012 give them an unwanted record in that they are the club with the most defeats in the Football League's Play-Off Finals. On the other hand, Glovers fans maybe getting a bit ahead of themselves might

want to note that means that they were capable of getting past the semi-final stages on four of those six occasions. Their overall record at this stage may explain some of the slightly world-weary reactions of Blades fans around the internet in the past week or so - the objective will be to try to extend that run to seven by the time we reach Monday tea time.'
Trouble is, it is those sort of records that have to come to an end sometime.

Friday 3 May somehow arrived. So did the expectation, the hope, the fear, the pumping adrenalin as the Green Army marched North.
The *Green Room II* site was full of posters predicting the score from 5-2 Yeovil to 4-0 Sheffield. Take your pick:
*Play Off Predictions.*
*I am unsure about tonight, as the thing with being confident, is the loss will then seem worse than it is.*
*I think a 1-1 draw or Sheff U will sneak it 2-1*
*However think we will win by 2 clear goals on Monday (Greenarmy28)*

~~~~~~~~

*On the way*
*Finished work for the day and en route. Feel like a kid night before Christmas! Buzzing . Had a dream last night. Game finished 0-3. Hayter, madden 2 coyg* (true glover)

~~~~~~~~

*If we can put in a performance like we did against the Blades at their place this season, we will be fine.*
*I am just glad it wasn't Swindle.*
*I have a funny feeling the winner between us and Blades will be playing Brentford at Wembley.* (Wurzel)

At Bramall Lane, Chris Morgan, Sheffield's caretaker manager claimed that they were the underdogs. That was nice, thanks for the compliment. Little Old Yeovil were officially the bigger club. The bookies begged to differ quoting odds of 11/10 for a Blades win, 3/1 Yeovil.
Gary had his view as well:
*We're not the ones who are expected to win it, either against Sheffield United or if we get through to the final. We're certainly going to be the underdogs. In that way, we're not the ones that are under pressure - it will be the other teams that are under pressure, because nobody expected us to be where we are.*

Gary had left nothing to chance in the preparation of the squad. He took them off for two days at the superb facilities of St George's Park to get them away from the pressures and a chance to work a bit of that Johnson magic on them:

*Well we feel that when there are big games, and we've done this before, people have to worry about tickets and making sure that their grannie has got a seat where she can see. So we're making sure that we do all that. We've done that, and so by Thursday when we go away it will all be done and finished, and we'll have two real good days together to sort of brainwash them really. I like to talk to them in meetings, and I want them to talk that meeting out onto the pitch from training. I want to eventually try to get them psychologically up for it, because physically they're up for it.*

A crowd of 15,262, including 1,023 Yeovil supporters turned up to witness this the first leg of the League One Play-Off semi final. Sheffield fans started the proceedings with a loud rendition of their 'Greasy Chip Butty'song and then seemed to forget that they should support their team for the next ninety minutes. Yeovil on the other hand outnumbered 14 to 1 sang their hearts out throughout the tense and hard fought match and gave great encouragement to the lads.

The hearts of those at the ground or back home watching the T.V., listening to the Radio, or live streaming on computers in far flung places across the globe, must have been pumped with pride and passion for the way Yeovil Town played. Every man of them gave their all, throwing themselves at everything in defence, sweeping the ball up the park with fast one touch passes, tough as nails but smooth as silk. If only they could have got the ball in the back of the net. A header off the line from Paddy Madden was as near as Yeovil came.

Sheffield, gritty, not much flair, had that one stroke of good fortune. A scrappy goal from their substitute, Callum McFadzean at the start of the second half was all that separated the two sides at full time.

A defeat, any defeat to any team in any competition is difficult to take but somehow this one was different. We had all seen the quality of the Yeovil team and knew that back at Huish Park, on Bank Holiday Monday 6 May, things could be so very different. After all it's was only half time.

GJ when interviewed afterwards was upbeat:

*"When it's two legs you're not out of it, that's for sure. I'm disappointed with how the goal came about and it probably wasn't a beautiful game. But we gave it a go after the break, showed a bit more bravery on the ball and had*

*our chances. We played our better stuff after the goal and being one goal down at Huish Park with our fans behind us making that noise I'm sure we can get that back."*                                         *"It will be very colourful and noisy. I've been telling the new lads, when this place has 8000 or 9000 in it then it feels a lot more because they are right on top of you. It is a game to look forward to and when it comes round everybody will be pleased with the effort everyone has put in. Me and the boys feel Monday can't come round quick enough. It will be all-action at Huish Park, and I'm really really looking forward to it."*

In fact just about everybody was upbeat:
*Although gutted to have lost in the manner we did whilst dominating for large periods of the game still feel that our "Little old Yeovil..." are more than capable of slaying yet another Giant to obtain a position once unthinkable.*
*Still have to pinch myself now and again when I look back in realisation of how far this great club has come in such a short time.*
*In Gary, (and the boys), we trust and here's to Monday and our just deserts.....* (Brizzol Glover)

~~~~~~~

*Our boys should be proud!*
*They put in a fantastic performance a should be proud!*
*We can do them on the return leg.*(Judd)

~~~~~~~

*Yea, just don't want that ' plucky boys nearly did it again  tag, I think it's there for the taking. We need a big noise from the 12th man on Monday* (Green MP)

In the other semi final, Swindon and Brentford drew, thereby giving us no further clues as to who we might meet (once we brushed Sheffield Utd aside of course)

On the eve of the second leg the bookies were putting Sheffield United as 2/1 favourites to win promotion, Brentford 11/5, Swindon 100/30 and poor old us 11/2. Well we all know how acurate the bookies are – relegation for us at the start of the season.

# CHAPTER 10

# WEMBLEY!!

Monday 6 May dawned bright and mild, deer scampered in the fields, birds sang gaily in the trees, jolly road sweepers were whistling a happy tune, could it have been 'Yeovil True'? All was well with the World!

Others were also up early for some reason:
*Morning campers*
*Well, this is it, this is our day. Thatchers Gold Stand needs to sing like never before, the rest of the stands will follow. The players are all looking forward to playing in front of a full house, let's be that twelfth man because we can do this, we can be the giant killers......"little old Yeovil"....bring it on.....!(Greenpiece)*

~~~~~~~

*Let's blow the roof off and be the 12th man! Anyone else feeling a tad sick? COME ON YOU GLOVERS!* (Pager)

By 1.30pm. The Hollywood script had been written:
All action heroes in beautiful green and white face up to giant northern bruisers in toothpaste red and white stripes.
Being 1-0 down the heroes must score quickly, 6 minutes should do it.
Kevin Dawson, ( Tom Cruise), slips inside the penalty box and plants the ball in the net. Camera pans to show 1000 stunned statues behind the net and then on to 7,000 delirious maniacs who have gone completely off their heads.
The action continues with a hard fought tussle between good and bad.
The bad guys bring on a 'super villain'(Alfred Molina – Dr Octopus) Dave Kitson. He tries a few crafty tricks but nothing goes for him.
The tension builds as extra time looms and maybe the green and whites will be forced to take penalties! Two of the heroes have other ideas.
Johnny Depp, playing Paddy Madden strokes a perfect lofted ball into the box and Henry Cavill (Superman), Ed Upson flies, as in' is it a bird is it a plane?' and connects sweetly with his head. Camera action follows the ball into the back of the net and onto those demented green and white fans.
No panning in this time on the other lot, scenes too shocking for the film, sobbing, wailing, falling to the floor.

There is just time for the cheeky heroes' supporters to chant "You're just a bus stop in Sheffield", a quick "Hey Gary Johnson" and a beautifully sung 'Que Sera, Sera, We're going to Wembley' before the final whilst blows. 2-1 to the heroes. Pan in on a steward saying "Keep off the Grass lads" before being engulfed by thousands scaling the walls and racing across the hallowed turf in celebration.

Usually the trouble with Hollywood is that their films are always too farfetched and over the top but by 3.15pm it had all come true and Huish Park was partying. The three Amigos, Gary, Tel and Dazza had hugged each other until they were consumed in the Tsunami. The players leapt into the Main Stand and bounced up and down in the Director' box. The directors bounced as well.
Flags, scarves, hats, babies were tossed in the air as the crowds sang and danced. WE WERE ON OUR WAY TO WEMBLEY!!!!

The celebrations rolled around to the beer tent where calls for" bottles of your finest Champagne" were heard but we settled for Thatchers Gold and a sausage roll. Folk stumbled about in a complete daze with silly smiles on their faces. If you'd come from another planet you would have thought you had landed at a 'funny farm'.

When sanity had been resumed and fans had a chance to look at the Sky T.V. footage, Peter Begrie was saying how 'Humongous' the achievement of Little Old Yeovil was. Karl Robinson, manager of the best team in the league, MK Dons thought we'd done alright as well. We love you to Karl. Did you like your banner? 'Karl Robinson – Who?'

When Gary Johnson emerged from the sea of boiling humanity he spoke in interview to BBC Bristol:
*"We've been talking about heroes and villains and there was a villain out there who turned into a hero which was fantastic. He (Upson) was one of those who had a bit of a lack of concentration in the first leg that led to their goal. He thought I might have left him out all week, along with a couple of others. But I gave those villains the chance to be heroes and that is what they did."*          *"Ed came up with something and credit to him. His mum and dad didn't call him Ed for nothing! I love them all to death and when I smack them I feel very sad, it is like smacking your little un, you don't really mean it! But I may have to smack them a bit more to get our promotion because we've come this far -*

*we have to get this promotion now."*                    *"When you've come this far you can't be this close to the Championship and blow it. We have beaten a big club in Sheffield United. Their lads on the day couldn't cope with the mentality and the mental toughness of our team."*

When the interviewer asked GJ how in felt, bearing in mind that 0-4 at Sheffield United was Gary's first game, he replied:

*I keep telling you - that was Terry's last game! That wasn't my first game! (laughs) Listen, let me just say about those two - and I know it was a great question - but really the answer that I want to give is that with Terry Skiverton and Darren Way, what a couple of hard working young lads they are. They've been fantastic. You couldn't do this on your own. I'm pleased for them, as they had to try to keep this club in this division for a long time. Now we've got together, and we've found a scenario and a commitment between us. We thought the players that we brought in would do the job or us - and they have done a job for us. Terry and Darren deserve as much credit as I have got.*

Ed (now Matt) Upson, having been misnamed by a Sky T.V. interviewer, said later that:

*"I could have kept running after that goal, I could have run straight out the stadium and run home. There was a bit of a tear in my eye. There were all sorts of emotions. I can't get my head around it just yet, it is something I'll have to go home and sit and think about for a while. My first ever header was earlier this season against Wycombe in the cup but they are a rarity and a great time to produce something that rarely happens. It is the most important goal I've ever scored in the biggest game I've ever played in, so to do that was special for me. I will hopefully score a more important goal in two weeks' time - the winner."*

To be honest not that many forum fans posted after the game. It's not easy to hit the right keys when you're drunk and still dancing. Those that could said:

*This club. The fans, the Manager, the Directors, the Chairman ----- what can you say? Unbelievable scenes at Huish Park today. This club is sooooooooooooooooo very special to my heart and many others and we have gained so many new fans today who hadn't been before. Achieve by Unity says it all. Well done to one and all. (garyjohn)*

133

~~~~~~~

*FORTRESS HUISH!* *What*
*an atmosphere today...massive crowd...positive attitude....I'm sure teams*
*hate coming to little old Yeovil!* ( Judd)

Congratulations poured in from across the globe, well Hartlepool, Cardiff
and Bristol:
*Congratulations!*
*From a Hartlepool fan! well played today. Best of luck in the final! hope you*
*beat Brentford.* (MonkeeHanger)
~~~~~~~
*Congratulations make amends for 2007 and win the final* (CardiffCityFan)
~~~~~~~

*Huge Congratulations!*
*Now make sure you go one better than we did with Gary, and enjoy the*
*great times while you can. You'll be looking back on this season with fond*
*memories for a very long time, especially if you can pull of that final result.*
*Fingers crossed and best of luck!* (bcfc fan)
~~~~~~~
*What ,no congrats from a*
*rooooooooooooooooooooooooooooooooooooooooooooooovers fan ?????*
(Green MP)

Despite the excitement we could not forget that over in West London a
battle was going on to decide who would have the honour of playing
Yeovil at Wembley. Brentford and Swindon were going head to head at
Griffin Park and it seemed when Brentford went 3-1 up that it was a
foregone conclusion but Swindon clawed it back to level on 95 minute.
Eventually a penalty shoot-out separated the two teams, 5-4 to Brentford.

Send out the invitations! Wembley Stadium has much pleasure in inviting
you to attend a football match, namely the League One Play Off Final
between Brentford and Yeovil Town on Sunday 19th May 2013, at 1.30pm.
Dress optional!!

In the forthcoming days the town buzzed, every conversation in the pubs,
the streets, the shops and over the garden fence was all about Yeovil.
Could they win and what would happen if they did? Was it possible for

such a tiny club on such a tiny budget to stand a chance against the massive clubs that stalked the Championship? Should we really try for it, we might be better off staying in league . We were sure to come straight back down. The vast majority were positive. Of course we wanted to win. Of course we wanted to be in the Championship. Let's ride the experience and enjoy every minute, win or lose.

*Ciderspace* very kindly printed a seating plan of the Wembley to help us all get the right tickets. *See Tickets* were going to be our on line website, prices between £30 - £80, plenty of tickets available. Form an orderly queue and go for it at 9.00am Wednesday 8 May. Some 12,000 were snapped up in the first 32 hours and by the time we got to Wembley around 20,000 proud Glovers were in attendance.

 After our less than inspiring performance both on the pitch and the singing in the stands, we wanted to get this one right. We had no worries about the team and how they would perform. 'In Gary we Trust'. It was the 12th man that was worrying some.
*Re: Wembley tickets*
*I really hope that this outside agency will have some sort of filtering system as to allow 'the singers' to sit together. The atmosphere was awful last time. (mll1986)*
Someone was listening because immediately blocks 109 – 114 on the East side were designated for the 'singers'. Excellent, one less thing to worry about. Now what about flags, drums and trumpets. Wembley had rules about such things. Despite hearing an almost full orchestra play when England are at home, it seems that you cannot take musical instruments into the stadium. If you wanted a drum you had to apply to a special dept. Banners apparently needed special staff to supervise them. Yes, even that 'Little Old Yeovil' one. Make your cheque out for £1,250 please!!
Some thought this a tad over the top:
*What a load of nonsense, although I'm delighted we have made it to Wembley I can't help feeling that this stadium milks each supporter to the hilt, from the price of a hotdog, the tickets and the price of having that little banner inside the ground. It really does take the pi$$.* (Green Machine*)*

~~~~~~~~

*Surely they are having a laugh? For that much you could hire a plane to fly over the stadium all game and fly the banner!* (Glover147)

Fortunately Wembley saw sense and 'Little Old Yeovil' did grace the arena.

Amongst all the 'raz a mataz' Darren Way was reflecting on how things had panned out for him as he spoke to BBC Somerset:

*"I was only thinking the other day, with the last four years of my life, I probably could never have dreamed of being in this position now. From once not walking, and then to being able to get out of the wheelchair, then taking my first steps, to being on a football pitch. Even if then my last steps were then picking up a trophy with the players, that would be a proud moment for me."*

*"Because the club have been very loyal to me, to give something back and bring success to the football club, which has never happened at this level, is what dreams are made of. I feel very passionate about the football club, and for them to be a Championship football club is what I've dreamed of, certainly since I've gone into management, even more than as a player. To have that success would stay with you for the rest of your life, whatever you achieve after that."*

May that success come your way Dazza.

One little thing that caught the eye of some was a congratulations announcement in the Sheffield Star for Friday 10 May:

**Edward James Upson**
Congratulations on
your recent success
-a hard earned and
much deserved 2-1
with honours.
Best wishes,
Dawn Seedy

Sheffield Wednesday fans love a good laugh at the expense of their near neighbours.

The *Green Room II* posters enjoyed it as well:

*Lovely girl Dawn - she's a wise old Owl herself. Very considerate of her to post such a message.* (Badger)

~~~~~~~

*Fantastically subtle. Love it!* (banio)

New replica strip was flying off the shelves in the Club shop, replacement stock was being drafted in and those still queuing after midnight were being given rolls and coffee (did I make that up?) One thoughtful lady, Pat Custard, who must be volunteer of the year, every year at Huish Park was concerned about people showing off those new shirts and yet keeping warm:

*GREEN & WHITE HOOPS - SHOW OUR COLOURS. Looking at the photos in the papers I recalled something that Geoff Twentyman said when he was at Huish Park covering one of our matches. He said that he had never seen a club's strip that stood out so much as ours and that the view of all our fans in the home terrace in their green and white hoops was quite intimidating to the opposition.*
*It got me thinking, that if the weather is not so clever at Wembley, fans may be tempted to wear something over their green and white shirts. Perhaps wearing something under the shirt instead to keep us warm would be the way to go, so that the maximum effect of the special green and white hoops can be seen? Yet another way we can support our boys!*
*That's the way I will be going anyway!! (PAT C)*

With an army of Pats' we could go far!

For most of us, sleepless nights were becoming the norm as we progressed to the big day and when sleep did come there were weird dreams about lifting the cup and then discovering you were a Brentford player, missing the coach or train and having to run all the way to Wembley and finding you had forgotten the ticket. Sunday could not come soon enough.

Someone else who was having dreams but hoping they would come true was Captain and hopefully lifter of the silverware, Jamie McAllister:

*"This time I'm captain and the chance to lift that trophy and be a winner at Wembley is all I've been dreaming about. Everyone wants to be captain and get to lift trophies in football. For the last couple of nights, that's all I can think about is getting up there to lift that cup. That's what I've been dreaming about for the last few nights. My little boy keeps saying to me as well that he just wants me to lift that trophy. I'm just desperate to get my hands on it, so I'm doing all that I can and I'm sure that all the boys and everyone involved are doing all they can to win it on Sunday."*

*"I was missing for a few weeks with my ankle and stuff like that, and I didn't think I was going to make the play-offs. But luckily enough, and thanks to (physio) Mike (Micciche) and the medical staff I got back and I got through the two games in the three days, and subsequently we're going to Wembley. I feel good and I'm raring to go."*

The team travelled up on the Thursday to keep them together and focused. Gary was not going to leave a single thing to chance, or so he thought. Just before they left for the Capital a news item burst forth declaring that Dan Burns had been involved in a road traffic incident. A newly qualified driver apparently mowed him down and left tyre marks on his leg. The question was, Why did you do it Paddy Madden? Why drive off before he had got his great long legs in the car? Fortunately Dan Burns was none the worse for wear and both legs would be in top condition for the Sunday match.

Our luck was certainly in, as once again Gary missed out on the Manager of the Month award With that curse avoided what could stop the Magic Johnson and his likely lads? On the Friday he took the squad to the stadium where they looked like Japanese tourists on holiday. They all took photos of each other and felt the velvety turf beneath their feet. Gary said: *"When we turn up on Sunday it's about doing a job. They won't be getting any cameras out, or doing any touristy things. That's why we're here. That's all today - Sunday is serious and we've got to win a football match. It's great that Wembley allow every team to do this, and to get a little bit of acclimatisation. You can see how the stadium is all on top of you. When the boys come out to play their game, they've to try to get rid of that surrounding, and just see the green grass and play their game. But what a fantastic stadium it is, and what a magnificent occasion for our club."*

Looking at the gigantic empty stands that were soon to be filled with Green and White supporters Gary said:
*"They'll help the players alleviate the fear of being at Wembley and making a mistake, because they'll be positive and I'm sure they'll sing their hearts out. I believe that since the last Wembley final, people have learned, so there's the Yeovil supporters experience that it was a bit quiet. So they've talked about singing blocks now, and I'm sure if those blocks get singing then they'll drag all the other ones along with them. That would be great. So they're massive to us."*

When asked about the size of the jump up to the Championship he answered:

*"You could say the biggest if you scientifically put everything together, because this club has come from the Conference, and it was a massive leap from the Conference to the League, and then from League Two to League One for our club. But it's an even bigger jump from League One to the Championship, because in the Championship you're playing teams every week that have been in the Premier League. That's an unbelievable situation for 'Little Old Yeovil' as they say."*

Sunday 19th May 2013 the team was announced.  They were:

**Marek Stech**
**2. Luke Ayling 5. Byron Webster 18. Dan Burn 3. Jamie McAllister (Capt)**
**22. Kevin Dawson 20. Joe Edwards 8. Ed Upson 14. Sam Foley**
**9. James Hayter 17. Paddy Madden**

**Substitutes:**
**12. Gareth Stewart 4. Richard Hinds 10. Gavin Williams 13. Vitalijs Maksimenko 15. Lewis Young 26. Matthew Dolan 29. Angelo Balanta**

These boys could write their names in Yeovil Town history and become immortalised in our Club's folklore. It's not a thing to be taken lightly.

Nor was the choosing of the right shirt to wear to the big occasion

*I realise it will be good for the club for people to buy the new shirt for our big day.*
*However I'm thinking Ill wear my 1992 FA Cup , Paul Sanderson No 7 shirt. I'm thinking it may be lucky.(Dorset GreenMan)*

~~~~~~~

*Torn between my "Welcome to Yeovil" Paddy Madden T shirt or the one that states "You can change your job, you can change your car, you can even change your wife but your club is for life! Yeovil Town" (Oracle)*

~~~~~~~

*My YTFC tshirt was purchased for Wembley 2007 and hadn't seen the light of day until last Monday. Has to be worn now as I think its luck has changed!*

*Edit; Mrs CJ offered to wash it when I got home on Monday, but I wasn't having any of that. (Cider Jaaarn)*

~~~~~~~

There appeared to be one that wasn't going to wear a shirt, just:
*Lucky pants, socks, scarf, flag and mug check nailed on win. (Das Boot)*
And very fetching you must have looked.

It was that lady again! Not content with sorting out the tea bars at Huish, preparing delicious ham rolls to sell to hungry fans and arranging the transport for the Devon & Dorset supporters, she was now trying to get us all to sing from the same song sheet! Having had long discussions on the *Green Room II* about what songs would be best to sing on the day, it was felt in order to encourage as many as possible, the words of one song should be handed out. Pat posted:
*Re: HELP NEEDED!!! DISTRIBUTING YEOVIL TRUE SONG SHEETS*
*The leaflets with the words for YEOVIL TRUE have arrived from OldGlover and I think they are FANTASTIC. He has done a really excellent job. They are like small green and white cards 15cm x 10.5 cm with words and chorus on both sides with a heading LEAGUE ONE PLAY OFF FINAL on the front and crest on the back. I think it is something all fans will want to keep as a memory of this fantastic occasion.*
*Now, I have a lot to get out, so are there any more volunteers for handing them out or those that are running coaches, can I get some to you?*(PAT C).

Folk stepped forward and before the match just about every Yeovil fan had a card in their hand in time for the massed choir to belt out our anthem with pride and passion. It just shows what team-work can do.

As we fell asleep on the night of 18th May many, religious or not, offered up a silent pray for a wonderful victory the next day. Little Old Yeovil had come so far, it would be a tragedy if they fell at the final hurdle.

The coaches were due to leave Huish Park at 7.00am and long before that a huge Green & White snake worked its way around the ground. This was a huge task getting all those thousands on the buses. Again hats off to those volunteers who got it sorted. Others caught the trains from Yeovil Junction and many more made the journey up the A303 by car. A smashing touch that must have fired everyone up, was a' Little Old Yeovil' banner proudly displayed on one of the overhead bridges.

Fans came from everywhere, New York, Dubai, Norway even Devon, some just squeaked it back from Aus, having missed the play-offs, others jetted in from Vegas (so flash) and one family came from Monacute (come on, cut me some slack, I had to have a mention somewhere). The Capital Glovers and others living in the London area had the tricky task of blending in with 20,000 Brentford supporters on the tube.

The Green Machine had arrived and flooded onto Wembley Way, stood beneath Bobby Moore's statute, posed for group photos and gave generously to the Prostate Cancer collectors.

Into the East Side as soon as the turnstiles opened, we stood slack jawed at the enormity of the arena, tier upon tier, even though many of us had seen it before. We were old hands after all, we knew our way around, we knew where to find our seats, find the beer and find BetFred and knew that at 11/1 Yeovil to win 2-1 was too good to miss.

And so the greatest match in the history of Yeovil Town unfolded. It was over in no time. We took the prize, thought by some to be worth as much as £4 million. The boys were magnificent. Yeovil supporters were magnificent. We hugged each other, we applauded one another. We were together as one.

We all have our individual memories of the stadium and the game but perhaps some of them are becoming a little hazy now. Why not flip back to Chapter 1 and indulge yourself again.

Like a giant green and white cloud we gently caressed London and then floated majestically towards our homeland in the West. Whoever we were, whatever we had done this would always rank amongst our finest days. The score, have I not mentioned it, 2-1. The bookies ran out of money when Yeovil fans went to collect next day.

Amongst all the joy there was sadness for the loss of one of our own. Nigel Strickland, life-long supporter, season ticket holder and member of the Cary Glovers passed away on the eve of the Final. R.I.P. Nigel. Your boys did you so proud.

With emotion breaking in his voice Gary spoke to Sky Sports: He said that hearing his club would play Championship football was music to his ears: *It sounds fantastic. It is a great achievement for our football club. This is for everyone who has been a part of it for ten years and certainly everyone who has been a part of it over the last year. I know what it is like to lose here, so*

*commiserations to Brentford. They give it a right go like they would do at Wembley, but we held out and I thought our supporters were absolutely magnificent and they saw us through the second half. So credit to them."*
*"It is one of them,(greatest moments) and right at this moment of course it is the best. But to have between 17,000 and 20,000 fans supporting us, which is a relatively small club, on a small budget, this is what you can do. So if you have got big ambition for a little man, you can get this."*
*I'm going to go and say well done again to the boys in the dressing room. I'm sure I've missed all of the spraying of the champagne, so that's handy because I've just bought this suit! (laughs) I had another one here just in case! So that's how much I thought we'd win it - I had another suit with me!*

The last laugh was on him as the lads tipped a large bin of icy water over that smart suit when he returned to the dressing room.

Terry Skiverton was equally chocked by the occasion when interviewed on the pitch by BBC Bristol:
*It's been a journey. It's a bit tough to talk right now, because I'm a little bit emotional with everything that's gone on with my career - the ups and downs. Sometimes you have to take a step backwards for the greater cause, and so for us to be here now I think is maybe a lesson for some other people. I'm not bigging myself up here, but if you put other things first, and you are somebody who is a little bit humble and you take that step (back), then other people and other things can then achieve.*
*I'm just so proud of my family and my mum. They're always there and I couldn't be any prouder of them than I am now. (pauses) I'm just going to go up there (to the Royal Box to lift the trophy) with the boys.*

Of course there weren't many fans who were capable of coherent thoughts after the game let alone posting anything. One or two who pulled themselves together put on the Forum:
*Wow*
*Just ecstatic, favourites for relegation and now we'll be playing against a team that's playing in Europe next season :O And my don't we deserve it (cfty)*

~~~~~~~

*Its official. Biggest pub team in England (whiteyfc)*

~~~~~~~

*What now for the club?*

*Will we*
*1/still have a marquee, probably*
*2/keep sir Gary, probably*
*3/survive a season in championship-hopefully*
*And finally, remain, the biggest small club of all time-of course.*
*I have to say today was one of the days of my life, I never thought, about*
*15years ago in the Isis league, we would get where we are now.*
*For this I thank GJ in the main-others have played a part, but the man*
*is the greatest Yeovil manager of all time.*(stewart.barnes)

Who wants Manager of the Month awards when you can have LMA Manager of the Season. The following night Gary Johnson was given this accolade by his fellow professionals at their awards dinner in London.

Yeovil Town went on to parade the Cup through the town centre of Yeovil and celebrated their victory with their people.

This little book began on 19May 2013 and went full circle and ended a couple of days later. In between was sandwiched the life of our football club, the highs and the lows. What we know is that another full chapter will begin very shortly and all that has been written here will drift away into history. A magnificent history that will be remembered for generations. Up The Glovers!!

# 2012-13 nPower League One Table

|   | | | Home | | | | | Away | | | | | | |
|---|---|---|---|---|---|---|---|---|---|---|---|---|---|---|
|   | Team | P | W | D | L | F | A | W | D | L | F | A | Pts | GD |
| 1 | Doncaster Rovers | 46 | 10 | 5 | 8 | 26 | 23 | 15 | 4 | 4 | 36 | 21 | 84 | 18 |
| 2 | AFC Bournemouth | 46 | 13 | 6 | 4 | 43 | 21 | 11 | 5 | 7 | 33 | 32 | 83 | 23 |
| 3 | Brentford | 46 | 14 | 6 | 3 | 37 | 22 | 7 | 10 | 6 | 25 | 25 | 79 | 15 |
| 4 | **Yeovil Town** | **46** | **13** | **4** | **6** | **36** | **22** | **10** | **4** | **9** | **35** | **34** | **77** | **15** |
| 5 | Sheffield United | 46 | 8 | 11 | 4 | 31 | 21 | 11 | 7 | 5 | 25 | 21 | 75 | 14 |
| 6 | Swindon Town | 46 | 10 | 9 | 4 | 44 | 15 | 10 | 5 | 8 | 28 | 24 | 74 | 33 |
| 7 | Leyton Orient | 46 | 13 | 3 | 7 | 31 | 20 | 8 | 5 | 10 | 24 | 28 | 71 | 7 |
| 8 | Milton Keynes Dons | 46 | 12 | 5 | 6 | 35 | 21 | 7 | 8 | 8 | 27 | 24 | 70 | 17 |
| 9 | Walsall | 46 | 10 | 8 | 5 | 38 | 29 | 7 | 9 | 7 | 27 | 29 | 68 | 7 |
| 10 | Crawley Town | 46 | 9 | 9 | 5 | 34 | 27 | 9 | 5 | 9 | 25 | 31 | 68 | 1 |
| 11 | Tranmere Rovers | 46 | 10 | 6 | 7 | 31 | 21 | 9 | 4 | 10 | 27 | 27 | 67 | 10 |
| 12 | Notts County | 46 | 9 | 6 | 8 | 32 | 26 | 7 | 11 | 5 | 29 | 23 | 65 | 12 |
| 13 | Crewe Alexandra | 46 | 12 | 3 | 8 | 26 | 22 | 6 | 7 | 10 | 28 | 40 | 64 | -8 |
| 14 | Preston North End | 46 | 8 | 9 | 6 | 31 | 22 | 6 | 8 | 9 | 23 | 27 | 59 | 5 |
| 15 | Coventry City | 46 | 7 | 7 | 9 | 29 | 27 | 11 | 4 | 8 | 37 | 32 | 55 | 7 |
| 16 | Shrewsbury Town | 46 | 9 | 7 | 7 | 29 | 27 | 4 | 9 | 10 | 25 | 33 | 55 | -6 |
| 17 | Carlisle United | 46 | 7 | 7 | 9 | 32 | 43 | 7 | 6 | 10 | 24 | 34 | 55 | -21 |
| 18 | Stevenage Borough | 46 | 7 | 5 | 11 | 26 | 34 | 8 | 4 | 11 | 21 | 30 | 54 | -17 |
| 19 | Oldham Athletic | 46 | 8 | 4 | 11 | 25 | 26 | 6 | 5 | 12 | 21 | 33 | 51 | -13 |
| 20 | Colchester United | 46 | 8 | 4 | 11 | 25 | 31 | 6 | 5 | 12 | 22 | 37 | 51 | -21 |
| 21 | Scunthorpe United | 46 | 7 | 6 | 10 | 31 | 38 | 6 | 3 | 14 | 18 | 35 | 48 | -24 |
| 22 | Bury | 46 | 6 | 6 | 11 | 24 | 33 | 3 | 8 | 12 | 21 | 40 | 41 | -28 |
| 23 | Hartlepool United | 46 | 5 | 8 | 10 | 19 | 27 | 4 | 6 | 13 | 20 | 40 | 41 | -28 |
| 24 | Portsmouth | 46 | 7 | 5 | 11 | 27 | 27 | 3 | 7 | 13 | 24 | 42 | 32 | -18 |